Manifestos

Planetarities

A short book series that investigates planetary troubles and proposes transformative approaches to planetary research and practice.

Manifestos

Édouard Glissant
Patrick Chamoiseau

Translated by
Betsy Wing and Matt Reeck

Goldsmiths
Press

Printed and bound by Versa Press, USA
Distribution by the MIT Press
Cambridge, Massachusetts, USA and London, England

Originally published in French as *Manifestes* © Editions La Découverte, Paris, 2021
Original (French) text copyright © 2022 Édouard Glissant and Patrick Chamoiseau
Translation (English) copyright © 2022 Elizabeth Wing and Matthew Reeck

A CIP record for this book is available from the British Library

This publication is a deliverable of The Seed Box program, which is funded by MISTRA – The Swedish Foundation For Strategic Environmental Research – and Formas – a Swedish Research Council for Sustainable Development.

ISBN 978-1-913380-54-0 (pbk)
ISBN 978-1-913380-53-3 (ebk)

www.gold.ac.uk/goldsmiths-press

Goldsmiths
UNIVERSITY OF LONDON

Contents

Series Foreword

By Jennifer Gabrys, Ros Gray, and Shela Sheikh

With multiple environmental crises erupting worldwide, the planetary has become a common topic. Yet while studies proliferate that speculate about the state of the planet or propose governance on a planetary scale, they often reinscribe dominant voices, knowledges, and ways of being. The *Planetarities* series seeks to unsettle prevailing engagements with the planetary by supporting work that grapples with the power dynamics, indeterminate relations, and poetic possibilities of eco-social transformations. Drawing on, extending, and reworking Gayatri Chakravorty Spivak's notion of "planetarity," the series takes up distinct types of "planet-thought" and "planet-feeling." For Spivak, planetarity was a concept that could undo the abstractions of globalism while expanding beyond isolated consolidations of self or identity. With "planetarities," this series further embraces the pluralistic concepts and practices that offer different connections and collectives tied to the planet.

As a series, *Planetarities* creates a space for work from writers and practitioners within and beyond Western and institutional contexts, with contributions from the Global South, Indigenous communities, and environmental activists working within transdisciplinary and transnational movements. This series seeks to advance theoretical and practice-based work as a plural and diverse collective project that shares a sense of urgency about planetary troubles. The texts in this series attend to planetary inhabitations and problems, from climate migration and environmental justice to multispecies world-building and the geopolitics of extraction. By considering how the planetary is at once summoned and unsettled through ecological and socio-political crises, the series poses a challenge to Anthropocene discourse by decentering the Anthropos and instead exploring how the planetary undoes and remakes humans and nonhumans as planetary subjects.

Manifestos, the first volume in the *Planetarities* series, presents just such a provocation and contribution to expanded planetary thought and practice. A translated collection of multi-authored manifestos and op-eds led by French-Martinican authors Édouard Glissant and Patrick Chamoiseau, *Manifestos* writes toward whole-world [*tout-monde*] relations from the perspective of what the authors name "small countries" with "big projects." The texts cover topics ranging from Guadeloupe, French Guiana and Martinique's relationship with colonial France to Hurricane Dean's impact in the Caribbean, Obama's presidency, and the necessity of poetics for any whole-world project. Together, they suggest how to confront and transform the challenges of colonialism, national identity, climate disaster, economic inequality, and environmental pollution – not as separate events but as interconnected conditions. For the authors, the "wholeness" of the world poses the challenge of addressing embroiled circumstances of abundance and want, reciprocity and justice, migration and flourishing. Connection is the baseline of being in the world. It is only by being in exchange with others – whether human, animal, or vegetal – that the whole world and its possibilities become possible as a dream and ongoing project. Since this is a poetic project, moreover, it requires beauty for its implementation. As Glissant and Chamoiseau write, "The Whole-World is sensitive to the warmth of utopia, the oxygen of a dream, the beautiful errantry of a poetics. It appoints art, and what art can divine, to rule over our global politics and the words we share." This is a planetary imagining written far from the gaze of a colonial globalism but close to the nerve center of pluralistic planetarities.

As a collection of short titles that tackle key topics of planetary relevance, the *Planetarities* series finds a supportive and like-minded community with Goldsmiths Press, which advances rigorous, experimental, and radical engagements with theory and practice. At Goldsmiths Press, we extend our sincerest thanks to Sarah Kember for her enduring support of the *Planetarities* series, and Ellen Parnavelas and Susan Kelly for contributing to the development and publication of the *Manifestos* text. In addition, we thank the original French-language publisher, La Découverte, for granting permission to undertake this translation. Betsy Wing and Matt Reeck created an impressive translation of the original *Manifestes*, and we are grateful to these translators for their excellent composition. Finally, this first volume of the *Planetarities* series benefited from generous support from The Seed Box program, funded by MISTRA – The Swedish Foundation for Strategic Environmental Research – and Formas – a Swedish Research Council for Sustainable Development. Contributions from The Seed Box members, including Astrida Neimanis, Björn Penrud, Cecilia Åsberg, Jesper Olsson, Katja Aglert and in particular Matthew Fuller, have helped to make this publication possible.

FOREWORD: AFTER ALL

"We can't let this go unchallenged!"

Édouard Glissant's capacity for indignation was true to the power of his poetics of being, on the same scale, relevant and vigilant. Relevant because it was unfailingly useful every day, called in some mysterious way toward the "state of the world" or one of the convulsions of the country of Martinique. Vigilant because, being both broad and deep, it brought a sensitive awareness to those always troubled areas of reality where both monsters and miracles occur.

These manifestos represented for him a chance not to deliver some truth or other, nor even to articulate a militant reply, but to stir things up on the subject of an event by bringing to it the most valuable form of inquiry: the one that has no question but that introduces an important distance to our perception of this thing which suddenly has become more complex.

They were also a gluttony.

They were gluttonous for reality when the exploratory lightning of a *Poetics of Relation* (that poem-mind) threw light on it, exposing it slightly and allowing us to distinguish a suddenly half-visible configuration of forces in the making, about which he could then engage in dazzling "recitations" – that almost magic word that has come down to us from the old creole storytellers, which has a wonderful way of ripping the veils of narrow realities wherein our ordinary thinking lies, and does this not to explain or teach us who knows what, but to weigh what it was in such a situation, such a world convulsion, such a twitch in our little country that, through that very convulsion, that very twitch, that situation, enlightened us. If our way of thinking produces the bubble of reality in which we live, think, and experience things, the poetic approach can pierce that bubble, so to speak, and move on (the way we seek a source) into unknown areas of reality, that unfathomable place where we still have to learn to stand upright.

They were also courageous.

His insurrection, by that I mean his thought, did not directly confront things that were unacceptable. (A poet isn't a militant; poetry serves only the vertiginous sense of being "outside.") It applied itself to what was unacceptable in order to unleash the still shivering lightning of expansion, a new vanishing point, a bright spot of "possibilities." Possibility is a bubbling up of the imagination, whose sense and above all its foolishness must be experienced; visibility is increased but, more than that, something invisible, something never thought and, above all, some fearless and unthinkable thing, the happening place of most of reality, is revealed. It takes courage to let go of the comfort of our old mentality and withstand all this.

"We can't let this go unchallenged!"
   That's how it all began.

We had no need to discuss the thing that was unacceptable any further, no need either to argue or agree about what had to be done. It was just a first shot, which I often wrote down – images, sensations along with the ideas that arose from those images and sensations ... That first draft would come back to me very quickly, taken apart and expanded by the extraordinary intertwining thoughts and words of the poet.

As for myself, I was always surprised every time to hear him rail against I don't know what indecency on the phone: *we can't let this go unchallenged!* Alarmed, I would try to figure out just what sort of weapons and divisions we had at our disposal, and just where he got the idea that it was possible for us to "do something," to *not let it go unchallenged* ... We were in a little dugout, maroons, and all we had was solitude, nakedness, and impossibility: *the things that writing maybe likes* ... So then I would write down a first draft the way a prisoner – perfectly aware of their powerlessness but still going to do it – makes a little weapon for themselves out of papier-mâché. The poet added wings, I would then add a scratch, and he would give it a refrain ... and we just liked seeing the thing take off ... After all these years during which I frequently contemplated those little migrations, the way these texts wandered on without a path about the contemporary matters of the world, I finally understood the importance he was giving "poetics," not as the force of "Power" but as "a power."

The entanglement of economic globalization and *worldness* (this unforeseen state of incredible mixtures and unanticipated individuations) produced the chaos-seed that is the Whole-World: an intemperate flood where only "becomings," as Deleuze called them, could be envisaged. Among these "becomings," there is the one (not yet attained) of a "more humane" relationship to the human condition, more humane at the very heart of existence, more humane in the more and more crucial urban, digital, and cosmic clash of ecosystems ... more humane in relation to the capitalist West's virulent qualities of absolutism and domination. There was also "Relation," the chaotic flow between everything and everything, between self and self, between self and Other, with the latter no longer the "foreigner," but everything that was "potentially becoming" in the lootings, humiliations, suppressions, age-old injustices. "Relation" has no morality: monsters prowl around in it as often as clustered miracles, but one can create a *conscience* there, one can grind the salt of an ethic on it and, above all, *one can, one must make it the wondrous work of our presence in the world!* This "becoming-in-Relation" exists in every human situation, every situation of existence – whether in those archaic colonial enclaves, which the Overseas Territorial Departments[1] continue to be, or in large urban ecosystems, or in the pervading digitalization, or the oceanic drawbacks of free markets, or even in the mental involutions where racism, xenophobia, Islamophobia, ethical failures, and insults to Beauty all fight over some lowlife fame ... Whether we wish it or not, this "becoming Whole-World" is there. It is a process that is also pervasive, granted to everyone, valid for everyone, and allows excess to spill over to a new level that needs it, far more than our old barbarities did, so everything can be seen from the banks (loved, tremulous) of *generosity-after-all.*

Poetics thus keeps watch in the adamant beauty of the world, in the unattainable density of reality. Fearlessly aquiver with a daring that is free of system, unwilling to share certitudes.

He can let nothing go unchallenged!

He embraces his times, he belongs to his times, deeply and unto death. This is the way he steps aside from them and, taking his distance from them as ever, thus receives (from bites of darkness and bitter nibblings) an oceanic youth: the youth that makes you want to get up and *do-something-after-all.*

Ho! My friends! No longer do I hear the voice of this old warrior, but I still hear every day the wonderfully vibrant one of a young poet who calls out to me: *Ah non! Gibier ho! We can't let this go unchallenged!* ...

Patrick Chamoiseau
Paris, February 27, 2020

---

[1] [Trans.] In French, DOM-TOM, or Départementes d'outre-mer, Territoires d'outre-mer.

MANIFESTO FOR A GLOBAL PROJECT: MANIFESTO FOR REFORMULATING FRENCH OVERSEAS DEPARTMENTS[1]

Édouard Glissant, Patrick Chamoiseau, Bertène Juminer, and Gérard Delver
January 2000

The entire world, and not just France, lies before us. If we, who live in Guadeloupe, French Guiana and Martinique, do not react to this new situation, if we do not enter with audacity and with speed into the debate before us, with its agreements and universal antagonisms, with its entirely pitiless and unpredictable rules, we will have no idea when it was that we ceased being motes of dust but became completely left out of this planetary game.

French Guiana is engaged in the same process of reworking its political and administrative status, despite its specific characteristics: its belonging to the continent of South America, the extensiveness of its land, the vertiginous diversity of its people with its significant populations of Amerindians, Africans, Asians and Europeans, the presence of an impressive international community in Kourou, the fact that it shares borders with the other Guianas and Brazil, countries with which it naturally shares a common future. Still, French Guiana fully recognizes its historical solidarity with Guadeloupe and Martinique.

Today, the statements of our political leaders concerning our present political and administrative status have made us look once again at this status. This is the moment to recall several principles that sum up our convictions,

---

[1] Published in the magazine *Antilla* (No. 867, January 14, 2000), then in *Le Monde* (January 21, 2000), the "Manifesto for a Global Project" (published originally under the title "Manifesto for Reformulating French Overseas Territories") is co-signed by Édouard Glissant, Patrick Chamoiseau, Bertène Juminer, and Gérard Delver. At issue is a proposal to reformulate the French Caribbean political system while reconceptualizing the situation there through a "global" approach. The "DOM," in French, or the "départements d'outre-mer."

since they are the tools we can use to make our uncertainties productive. It is perhaps also the moment to share with others our convictions and the experiences upon which they are based, as a type of offering.

A "people" does not develop in the context of collective irresponsibility

Without a doubt, the granting of the status of a *département* began to transform our lands through modernization, a higher standard of living and the general improvement of living conditions and social relations. But it also has become a crutch. A prevailing syndrome of habituated dependence and numbness has grown in concert with the increased presence of social welfare programs. To this list we must also add the general sense of being downtrodden and the undermining of local powers, which see themselves rendered powerless every time some great state commissioner arrives, bearing subsidies, making decisions. There's also this out-of-control consumption, which drives us to distraction and makes us forget about investing, about having goals for ourselves, about building a future. Consumption's endgame is only more consumption, which will lead eventually to the consuming of those who are bound to it. This is the challenge in front of us, and today even those who are in favor of assimilation need to reconsider what terrible things this may lead to.

Through granting the status of a *département*, France gave us access to its world.

Now we, by ourselves, must gain access to the world at large.

An administrative status cannot act as a people's living soul

Every administrative status is a tool used to implement an intention, desire, or gesture in the world. Of course, the struggle to change administrative status is legitimate. But this complex endeavor is born from what we would call a "project." The project is not programmatic. It is first and foremost a strategy, a dynamic frame for the realization of our hopes and dreams. It gives shape to every desire, intention, and gesture. It links people's energies and wills. It creates collective freedom that sustains each individual freedom, which in turn provides sustenance for the whole. Because it truly enjoys the full backing of everyone, this project is exempt from unilateral decisions, autocratic whims and the sterile, kneejerk reactions of institutions. And it is the project itself that generates these sites of power, these possibilities, which in turn make a certain juridical context inevitable. It is the project that produces the administrative status that is necessary for it, and not the reverse. Where the project is set aside in favor of the singular and unequivocal goal of attaining a certain administrative status, we have witnessed the persistence of dependence and reliance upon state handouts. Even in the instances where localities have been granted a larger share of administrative responsibility, we have seen the rise of nostalgia and calls for the reactivation of colonial rule. We have seen how the aborted gesture fails to actualize the space that was given to it. The autonomy of thought, the sovereignty of the imagination, the freedom of the spirit: these are the essential conditions.

In calling for the envisioning of a realist utopia of this sort that would accompany and support the fight for any new administrative status, we are invoking, in fact, the first freedom necessary for all other freedoms to be imagined: the freedom of thought. A free mind is first concerned with finding a way to bridge energies, desires, intentions, and to give them some meaning that does not need to be unique, but must be broadly pertinent. For a people, the ability to define a global project is the sign that the community is already free and that, strengthened by this freedom, it is ready to define the scope of its freedoms.

Without a doubt, our inability to conceptualize or bring to life a project is the result of being trapped in departmental status, which mires our imaginations in solutions that involve dependence and state welfare, solutions that pose problems for us and that make us unproductive. Dependence on social welfare makes any resistance impossible. It invalidates intuition just by preventing the implementation of realistically effective tools. This system excludes everything that does not conform to its law, everything that is not conducive to its rule. And it shows itself to be incapable of understanding or admitting the need for the least bit of audacity. It proliferates in this way until it asphyxiates itself. As it gradually wears itself down, this system nevertheless generates ever new impulses by which, paradoxically, it maintains itself. Demanding a certain administrative status without having envisioned a global project is, from our perspective, nothing more than another impulse to sustain the status quo.

It is not a crucial step toward a new beginning.

A pre-structured freedom eventually destroys freedom

There is no debating that it would be scandalous to avoid acknowledging the work of those politicians and bureaucrats who have long worked within the system and who, moreover, having confronted the impasses of this system, are now calling for us to move beyond it, in piecemeal ways or through whole-sale changes. But freedom cannot come from above. It emerges from within. What is received passively keeps us in the role of the subjugated. And so we see the advent of a new discourse in our political debates: that of nationalist assimilationism, which speaks of the country in every breath, but in doing so destroys it all the more. In this instance, the role of France should not be to decide the rubrics for our freedom, even after consultation, but to open what was closed, to unblock what was blocked, to oxygenate areas where asphyx-iation was allowed. Let us out of the bag constituted by departmental status. Unleash sovereign spaces likely to grow and evolve on their own. Standing here on top of the trash heap of failed solutions, we conclude that the only advances that will mean anything will be those that we ourselves come up with, which will put into play closely connected vertical structures that stead-fastly support the reality of freedoms.

To agree upon a project that unites us all is a foundational act

What can we do together to mark our existences in the world? How can we reconcile our necessary collective responsibility with the economic realities universally and ferociously dominating us? The time has come to publicly debate what many of us have thought separately.

The positive transformation of the economic and social fabric of Guadeloupe, French Guiana, and Martinique cannot be accomplished with-out the implementation of a global project that will look toward the future while bearing in mind the present.

Our countries cannot imagine the solutions to put in place, or when this ought to happen, from the perspective, for example, of massive industriali-zation, commercial agriculture, luxury tourism or the growth of the service sector, consumer culture, and so on. In all these cases, we are already too late, and what will be impossible has already been established.

Our only possibility is that of diversified, value-added production (value-added production being the mechanism whose exploitation produces real profit and real development) like those that have been put in place in most small countries that today have control over their futures. In the baroque con-cert of the world today, we believe in the future of small countries. In other words, we believe that there are no small countries; there are only big projects.

The general conditions of the West Indies, in French Guiana, and in the Caribbean (collectively, islands and areas that can easily be cleaned up and transformed) give rise to our belief that our value-added products would be tied to organic production, whose demand is increasingly irresistible in the world market. We must occupy this slot.

That is why some of us proposed long ago that we adopt in Martinique the global project of an economy centered on various organic products, and that we brand ourselves in the world market as "Martinique, an organic country," or "Martinique, foremost organic country in the world."

We call on all people of Guadeloupe, French Guiana, and Martinique to consider the need for such an orientation, even if a project of this sort may take on different forms in each of these countries – for example, through technology in French Guiana.

The difficulties of an organic project are staggering, and only some of a very general nature are listed here.

A project such as this cannot be imposed from above. It would have to be everyone's business, and everyone would have to play their part in fighting for it. It will not be viable if any part of our reality, however small, does not participate or is excluded by any means or prejudice whatsoever.

It will not be viable without the involvement of the youth, who will lend to it both enthusiasm and action. Without a collective intention and a common objective, the goals of social integration and employment are unrealizable.

It will not be viable if it does not promote cultural, linguistic, and artistic movements in our streets and in our hearts, which can awaken our minds and renew our ways of imagining ourselves and the world. This project will not be viable if it is not holistic – that is, if it does not encompass all sectors of activity, agriculture, tourism, agrobusiness, medicine, fisheries, communication, the fight against pollution, the education system, the production and consumption sectors, and so on. Any organic undertaking that remains isolated is fragile and likely to fail.

It will not be viable if it does not arrange for a step-by-step implementation schedule for the transformations in store. Realistic caution and the audacity of the global concept operate in tandem. It will not be possible to develop this project in an isolated way, cut off from the efforts and solidarity of the other countries of the Caribbean, or from French Guiana's South American neighbors. When united in solidarity, this area should come to represent one wellness zone on earth.

That said, there are already thousands of specific problems to be addressed by our determination and patience. We suggest that the axes of development of a project such as this be studied, opened up for discussion and public approval, and presented to public officials, unions, economic actors, educators, artists and cultural doyens, youth leaders and sports figures, public health workers ... to all participants of civil society, who will be tasked with carrying out the project.

We are convinced that if this global project does not gain universal support, it will still be necessary to invent another, which would have to be based, as well, upon the need for a value-added production. It is in this way that the openings of political freedom will cease to be just so many broken promises. And it is a project such as this that will also prepare us to better define and clarify the areas that we must overcome.

Self-organization generates a living fabric essential for all peoples

Dependence in and of itself is not what most heavily shackles the spirit of freedom. And, moreover, who in today's world can escape dependence and interdependence? No, dependence is lethal when it does not create any space for self-organization. Self-organization is the birthright of every living being. Decentralization, whether of an enlightened variety or not, does not allow any possibility for self-organization. Decentralization cannot support the arrival of a new organism. It is the same for autonomy, which is locked inside the horizons of its administrative status and its need to recognize the governmental center from which this autonomy was granted. Decentralization and autonomy will be lifeless if they do not become projects that exceed their self-limitations.

Sovereign space becomes the inevitable result of a global project, and it alone can support the new and the unexpected in the unfathomable combinations of the living organism, which evolves and builds through its own momentum. Sovereign space alone allows for a type of self-organization that is not reduced to provisional self-governance.

In the interactions between organic dependences, necessary interdependences and the practice of self-organization, freedom is at work.

This expands the possibilities. It introduces give-and-take into the system, allows for interaction among initiatives, innovations, choices, strategies, first attempts and new beginnings to interact. Politics, in its truest sense, is introduced into the governing structure, which must then figure out how to stay in balance. What makes departmentalization a vicious tool is that there is no play in its workings. Choice, invention, and political adventure are routed into ready-made dead-ends. We do not pretend to speak for everyone. And so we do not ask for freedom to arrive from on high, or from a definitive administrative status, or from a legally binding decision, or for the keys to be handed over to us. But, after more than four centuries of colonization, slavery, and departmental domination, we challenge France to acknowledge its responsibilities.

In partnership with France, and linked through undying mutual affection, we want to see presented before us the specific possibilities of choice, of creative contact, of promising alternatives, of the necessity of travel and invention – all things that, in their activation, kindle the freedom of the spirit.

We reaffirm that the status of our status, or the direction it will take, lies in creating the conditions for the emergence of the global project we envision, which will, in turn, fundamentally break the ecosystem of dependence and state welfare apart, producing a decisive transformation that will allow for self-organization.

And so it is the people of Guadeloupe, French Guiana, and Martinique who decide how to administer their land and their sky, and who decide on questions of instruction, teaching, justice, and health.

It is the people of Guadeloupe, French Guiana, and Martinique who decide for themselves about their role in the fabric of Caribbean life, or South American life, or their role in the social, cultural, and economic dynamics of the Americas. They should be allowed to directly access international institutions that regulate business across the world, as well as European or other entities operating in the world.

It is the people of Guadeloupe, French Guiana, and Martinique who define and appropriate the financial resources, as well as other types of resources, which will be necessary for the functioning of their project.

It is the people of Guadeloupe, French Guiana, and Martinique who institute in each country, through popular vote, a new assembly entrusted with powers in the abovementioned areas of commerce and life. This assembly would name an executive with the power to activate well-defined policies and guidelines for the global project accepted by our peoples.

This assembly is to be our site of self-organization, in partnership with France and based upon mutual respect, true exchange, and brotherly sharing.

MSR

FROM AFAR ...: OPEN LETTER TO THE FRENCH MINISTER OF THE INTERIOR ON THE OCCASION OF HIS VISIT TO MARTINIQUE[1]

Édouard Glissant and Patrick Chamoiseau
December 2005

Martinique is an old land of slavery, colonization, and neocolonization. But this endless sadness is a valuable teacher: it has taught us exchange and sharing. Dehumanizing situations have this valuable side to them: they preserve in the hearts of the subjugated the shudder that rises to become the call for dignity. Our land is a country that most fervently desires that dignity.

It is inconceivable that a nation in the world today would close itself off with such tight identitarian strictures, ignoring what is now creating world community: the serene will to share the truths of the past that we hold in common and the determination to share, too, the responsibilities of the world to come. The greatness of a nation has nothing to do with its economic or military strength (which can only be one means of guaranteeing its freedom). What makes a nation great comes, instead, from its ability to weigh the course of things in the world, to apply itself when the ideas of generosity and solidarity are threatened or when they are weakening, always in order to bring about, in the short and long terms, a future that is truly common to all peoples, whether they are powerful or not. It is inconceivable for such a nation to propose a law (or to impose one) concerning the direction instruction must take in its educational establishments, taking a trick from the bag of authoritarian

---

[1] This text was uploaded to the internet as an open letter to Nicolas Sarkozy, who was then the Minister of the Interior, upon his visit to Martinique in December 2005. It addresses the intense polemics unleashed during the second term of Jacques Chirac, specifically what happened in February 2005 after a law was passed that intended to justify the role and the positive effects of colonization. (This law was repealed in 2006.)

regimes, inconceivable that this pedagogical mandate would aim directly at masking its responsibilities in an endeavor (colonization) that benefited it in every possible way and that is in every possible way irrevocably deplorable.

The problems of immigration are global. Poor countries, the points of origin for immigrants, are becoming poorer and poorer. And rich countries, which once welcomed these immigrants, often arranging for them to come to meet their labor needs – and, it should be said, thus practicing a type of slave trade – have perhaps today reached the threshold of saturation and now turn toward a selective slave trade. But the wealth created by these examples of exploitation has generated infinite forms of poverty in almost every corner of the world, thus causing new rounds of migration. The world is a whole. Abundance and want cannot pretend that the other does not exist, especially if one causes the other. The proposed solutions are not drastic enough to meet the severity of the problem. Governments choose one of two general approaches: the politics of integration (as in France) or communitarian politics (as in England). But in both cases, the immigrant communities, abandoned with no resources in unlivable ghettos, have no real means of participating in the life of their host country and can only participate in their home cultures in a partial, guarded, and passive way. These cultures become, in certain cases, cultures in the process of disappearing. None of these governmental choices proposes a true politics of Relation, which would consist of: the frank acceptance of differences, without the immigrant's difference being attributed to some form of communitarianism; the implementation of global and specific types of social and financial procedures, without that leading to the creation of a new classification; and the acknowledgement of the interpenetration of cultures, without there being a dilution or disappearance of any of the diverse populations brought in contact. Locating a balanced position within these coordinates without losing sight of the world's horrors, however, would be truly one of the beauties of the world.

If each nation does not abide by these essential principles, then the ways people are classified based upon appearance, the well-intended forms of discrimination, the quotas that shield people from culpability, the religions bankrolled by secularism run amok and all the outpouring of aid to the human masses of the Global South, who are still the victims of the old power structure, will only touch the world glancingly, without truly confronting the problem. Moreover, these measures make for the conditions of daily repatriations, detention centers, rewards for policing, the triumphant tally sheets of annual expulsions. These are theatrical responses to threats that they invent for themselves, or that they wave menacingly to scare people away. These are the barriers imposed by an approach that remains oblivious to the real world.

No social situation, even the most degraded one – and especially that – can justify harsh incivility. When face to face with a life, even when that life is but dimly perceived within the precedents of one of the most oppressive lineages in judiciary history, there is always first and foremost the overwhelming reality of distress: it is always about a human being, most often crushed by the logic of economics. A republic that offers a work pass in fact opens its door to a human dignity in which lies the right to think, to commit errors, to succeed and to fail, just like all living beings. This republic can also mete punishment, according to its laws, but in no case can it take back what has already been given. The gift that is partial, the welcome that demands a bowed head and silence, are closer to segregation than integration and are always very far from human.

The world gives us the gift of its complexities. From birth, each of us is an individual, the holder of several forms of identity, without being reducible to any one among them. And no republic can flourish without harmonizing the expressions of these multiple forms of identity. These relation identities still have a hard time finding their place in out-of-date republics, but what hostility they lead to is often translated into the desire to participate in an alternative republic. Republics that are "one and indivisible" must cede place to unified, complex republics whose complexity prepares them to incorporate the diversity of the world into their existence. We believe in a global treaty that provides a platform for "natural" nations (nations still without statehood, like ours) to find their voice and express their sovereignty. No act of memory can, by itself, prevent the return of barbarity: the memory of the Shoah needs the memory of slavery, as it does all other memories. Forms of thinking that reject this are insults to thought. The smallest, most understated act of genocide stares at us and threatens us as much as it does multi-trans-cultural societies. The great heroes of national history must now admit that they participated in acts of virtue and also acts of horror. National memories are now subject to the truths of the world, and living together is only possible today in equilibrium with the truths of the world. Contemporary cultures are cultures living in the presence of the world. Contemporary cultures have value only to the extent that they welcome in the cultural vibrancy of the world. Identities are open, fluid, and flourish only through their ability to "change in changing" within the energy of the world. A thousand clandestine acts of immigration, a thousand arranged marriages, a thousand bogus family units should not prevent taking the just stance, which is welcoming and open. No fear of terrorism should be able to make us abandon the principles of the respect for privacy and the freedom of the individual. There is more blindness in a surveillance camera than there is political intelligence, more lingering menace than social or human generosity, more inevitable regression than real progress toward security …

It is in the name of these ideas, in view of these principles alone, that we are ready to welcome you, from afar, but in good faith, to Martinique.

MSR

DEAN CAME THROUGH: WE MUST REBUILD. APRÉZAN![1]

Édouard Glissant and Patrick Chamoiseau
August 2007

A hurricane came through. In its wake: the devastation of plant life, every sort of destruction and the desperation of those who are the poorest and most powerless ... But chaotic moments are often times of regeneration.

Every regeneration emerges from disruption. The more severe the disruption, the deeper the ensuing renewal can go – even sometimes to the extent of mutation. Nature knows how to use these times of collapse to experiment with unprecedented forms of vitality: trees come back with great vigor as they recover from their trauma, and when the ravaged ecosystem dusts itself off, it redistributes possibilities of varying intensity.

In fact, disaster or crisis presents, above all, opportunities. When everything collapses or finds itself upended, both things that are firmly entrenched and those considered impossibilities find themselves shaken around. It is the improbable things that new light suddenly reveals. It is the forbidden things, the loose, lazy, and sterile habits that cry out for relief. What is true for the natural world is also true for cultures, peoples, identities, and civilizations.

---

[1] This text, published in *Le Monde* on August 25, 2007, followed the passage of Hurricane Dean through the Caribbean archipelago. On August 18, Dean devastated Martinique. [Trans.] *Aprézan* is a creole word that indicates "now" in many different ways. It is not annotated in the French because the ear accustomed to metropolitan French can easily hear "à présent" in it: presently, at this moment, currently, immediately, right now ... I have occasionally added words in this translation that direct its meaning, but I have just as frequently left the creole word to speak for itself.

It would be absurd if all we gained from the crisis was some moaning and groaning or a shudder of fear. It would be a pity to do less than does the most elementary biotope, less than the animals, simply to restore the order that was disordered by the crisis.

As if the tree, rather than devoting itself to putting out new foliage and impatient branching, were to flail about, mourning and seeking the trees that had succumbed to the wind. In a few days there are new sprouts. The birds will have moved their nests. Tomorrow everything around will quiver with germination and new beginnings. In every crisis, right from the start, there is a now that opens – an *aprézan*.

Aprézan to profit from this calamity to rehabilitate what one can. *Aprézan* to clarify. *Aprézan* to reconsider. *Aprézan* to keep shining a light on the places where ruptures and breakage have opened up possibilities. Every rebirth is priceless, there is no rebirth that is useless or trivial. Every restoration emerges from a fog of an infinite number of revivals ...

Perhaps it is the *aprézan* to take advantage of the fact that half of the billboards are down. They used to cover up our landscape but it is perhaps the *aprézan* for us to plan for more restrictive regulations.

The *aprézan* to bury all the electric wires that can be buried. The *aprézan* to encourage cisterns in homes and solar energy ... Perhaps it is the *aprézan* to review our relationship with the great, old trees, to understand the extent to which age fills them with mystery and magic, how much they are a natural inheritance that is priceless, to understand that any tree that lives a long time maintains and cares for itself, prunes and feeds itself, and only falls or comes apart when it is neglected. It is even the *aprézan* for the seashores where one can imagine some radical reorganization.

But a more important *aprézan* concerns agriculture, particularly bananas. Production of bananas constitutes the backbone of our odd economy. A fragile green thing, the banana tree is uprooted by even the slightest gust of wind; it is the source of soil and groundwater infestations, and is loaded with pesticides. What it brings in as business is practically nothing in these days compared with how hard it is to find good food.

Fields of them have been laid low and distress calls are increasing, overestimating the need repeatedly in order to demand supplementary payments, one more government subsidy, additional aid, the umpteenth rescue package. The loud, expert claims are indeed understandable because, supposedly, thousands of people depend on the product. And we are aware of that.

Those thousands of people are never the ones who benefit the most from the bounty handed out. But those thousands of people deserve more consideration than they are ever given by the people cheerfully calling for subsidies. Those who, by the same token, are reproducing the hellish cycle of dependence that supports a product with no future, aid that perpetuates a pernicious system. There is no *aprézan* in that sort of compassion. In responding to the emergency, what is essential has been forgotten. Above all, what is forgotten is something that no logical politics ignores: nothing is more urgent than what is essential.

It is in the name of those thousands of jobs, all that despair, that it is crucial to dare *aprézan* – by thinking, imagining, looking ahead and desiring a future, now in this moment. Renouncing the massive subsidies, renouncing the truckloads of well-meaning aid – why allocate that to simply restarting this cycle of dependence? Why not use it as the breath of rebirth and commit it to a critical restructuring? Why not specify that this is the moment – an *aprézan* that is short term, one that is long term and one that is ongoing between the two – to get away from an agriculture dependent on pesticides in favor of an agriculture that is reasonable and principled, opening up to a completely organic form of agriculture?

Why not outline an *aprézan* of cleansing the soil and reconverting it that would in less than 20 years move Martinique closer to goal of having an organic planet (blue Martinique, pure Martinique, land of regeneration and health, land of nature and beauty …) that we have been recommending for a decade and that other countries near us already envision?

A thousand square kilometers, it can get hold of itself, get its act together, it can clean itself up, be in control, abide by a clear commitment, a global intention that would breathe new life into us and above all bring us into the world. *Aprézan.*

BW

WHEN THE WALLS FALL: NATIONAL IDENTITY BEYOND THE LAW[1]

Édouard Glissant and Patrick Chamoiseau
September 2007

One of the richest but most fragile aspects of identity – both personal and collective – and one of the most precious as well is that, clearly, identity develops and gains strength continuously: nowhere do we find identitarian stasis. Also, it can neither be formed from nor find justification in rules, edicts or laws, which would authorize the nature of identity or guarantee its perpetuity by fiat. The principle of identity materializes or dematerializes, often in phases of regression (in a loss of a sense of self) or of pathology (in the intensification of a collective sentiment of superiority), whose various "cures," as well, do not issue from preordained, programmatic decisions mechanically applied.

Let us take a moment to consider this complex multiplicity, that we never see in its entirety, or all at once, which we call identity. An individual or a group of people can be conscious of the fluidity of their identity, but cannot control it in advance, by policy or principle. A Ministry of Identity would be impossible to manage. With such a ministry, collective life would become mechanical, as in a laboratory experiment, and its future would be antiseptic, rendered infertile by fixed regimens. Identity is first and foremost *a-being-in-the-world*, as philosophers say, more than anything else, a risk that we must accept. It furnishes a relation to the other and to the world at the same time as it results from this connection. It is this ambivalence that

---

[1] Text published for the first time by Éditions Galaade and the Institut du Tout-Monde in September 2007 in the context of the establishment, during the five-year presidency of Nicolas Sarkozy, of the creation in May 2007 of a Ministry for Immigration, Integration, National Identity and Co-development, headed first by Brice Hortefeux, then Éric Besson, during François Fillon's first stint as Prime Minister.

grants us both the freedom to start something and, subsequently, the audacity to change.

National identity

In the West, beginning in Europe, collectivities have been constituted in nations, whose double function was to exalt what were called the "values of the community," to defend them against all external aggression and, if possible, to propagate these values in the world. Thus, the nation became the nation-state, and gradually established the model that defines the interactions among modern world peoples. The community of a nation-state knows why it lives together, though it is never able to express this by thesis or theorem. It is due to this reason that the community expresses its shared life through symbols (its vaunted values), to which it attributes universality. This organizational model is the basis for colonial conquests: the colonizing nation imposes its values and claims an identity secured from all external threats, which we will call a unique root identity. Even if all colonization is principally economic exploitation, none can avoid this hyper-valorization of identity that justifies exploitation. The *unique root identity*, therefore, always needs to reassure itself through reinscribing itself – or at least trying to do so. But this model is also found if not at the origins, then at least in the first stages, of anticolonial struggles: mirroring the colonizer's example, oppressed communities found the strength to resist by claiming a national identity. In this fashion, the model of the nation-state spread throughout the world. Disaster upon disaster has followed.

From such reasoning, or from shared experience, we can conclude two things. First, newly minted nations, or ones that have changed regimes, have difficulty moving toward a conception of the nation that is free of a rigid and exclusive identitarian imperative. It seems to us that only post-Apartheid South Africa has expressed the inevitable need of an organization of voluntary mixing, of an ideal of exchange, which is not dictated by decree or governmental intervention, but where Blacks, Zulus, Whites, Coloreds and Indians can live together, without oppression and conflict: the invocation of a relation identity that would go further than the mere juxtaposition of ethnicities or cultures that we now call multiculturalism.

Second, it is only when the nation-state's existence is threatened that, inevitably, national identity consolidates as a weapon of defense (and deciding who is and is not a traitor to the nation) or as a spur to collectivization without needing to legislate this identity. But how can we believe today that the French nation is in any such danger, and that the influx of two or three thousand illegal immigrants from poor African countries constitutes the obdurate core of this menace? It seems to us that the active resistance to this influx reflects, more than anything, a preoccupation of an ideological order rather than any economic or practical rationale, or considerations for the commonweal.

We heard about a prodigy, a young conductor, who was born in a parking garage; his parents were practically homeless, immigrants and likely subject to deportation laws. People have assured us that the young boy who fell from a window trying to flee from the immigration police was among the best students in his class. In the name of a fixed notion of identity, will France coldly renounce all these suddenly under-appreciated and yet ultimately enriching things that diversity, the unforeseen, and the richness of the world are likely to bring to it? Or will it try to maintain some illusory control over it?

To make-world

Now, well in the twenty-first century, a great democracy, an old republic, the so-called birthplace of human rights brings together the following terms under the purview of a ministry designed primarily for repression: immigration, integration, national identity, co-development. In this concatenation, these terms collide, cancelling each other out, condemn each another, yet in the final analysis they register only a hint of regression. In this ministry, France betrays an unalienable part of its identity, one of the two fundamental aspects of its connection to the world (the other was colonialism): the exaltation of freedom for all.

It is true that democratic space is a field of antagonistic, extremely virulent forces. It, the least bad of all systems, demands constant attention and something like a soldier's vigilance. It is true, as well, that we have renounced the idea of the unerring progress of human consciousness, and that we have learned that regression and advancement are, practically speaking, inseparable: there, where the light burns brightest, shadows grow as well. It is true, as well, that the twenty-first century is the time when the world is making the world through the troubling auspices of economic liberalism: this capitalist virulence that co-opts the spirit of freedom and transmogrifies it into a structure that thrusts the strong and the weak, the haves and have-nots, and the able and the unable, into the gaping Gehenna of the "market." The systematization of the spirit of freedom is no longer freedom. It is a type of general disintegration, which exposes everyone, alone and powerless, to the appetite of the monster.

It is also true that in the free market, this "world-market," this "market-world," the gaps that emerge between shortages and abundance bring about intense migrations, like cyclones, which no border can hold back. *Homo sapiens* is, by definition, a migrant, an emigrant, an immigrant. We scattered across the world in this way, we took control over the world in this way. And in this way we surmounted sand and snow, mountains and chasms, and left areas of famine in search of food and water ... "There's no border that we won't cross ..." This can be verified by millions of years of history. It will be like this until the end (even more so with the climatic cataclysms on the horizon), and none of the walls going up everywhere around us, justified in whichever ways – yesterday in Berlin, today in Palestine or along the Mexican–American border, or in the laws of rich countries – will be able to suppress this simple truth: the Whole-World becomes more and more the house of everyone – *Kay tout moun*, in creole; it belongs to everyone, and its equilibrium is balanced on the fates of all.

Walls and relation

The temptation of walls is not new. Each time a culture or a civilization fails to succeed in conceptualizing the other, in conceptualizing itself along with the other, in conceptualizing the other that lies within itself, these unbending structures of rock, iron, barbed wire, electric fencing, and closed ideologies have been erected, have collapsed and then have returned again, carried in on the back of the moment's vituperations. These scared rejections of the other, these attempts to neutralize the other's existence – even to deny it altogether – can take the form of legislative cinching, the allure of an indefinable ministry or the fog of a belief transmitted through many media outlets, which, abandoning once and for all the spirit of freedom, act only to expand their control in the shadow of the powers that be and the forces that dominate society. And so a wall can be unofficial or official, modest or spectacular.

The very notion of identity has long acted as a wall: mark off what is yours, distinguish it from what is the other's, to which we attribute a hidden threat, a trace of barbarity. The identity wall has produced endless confrontations between peoples, as well as empires, colonial expansions, the slave trade, the atrocities of American slavery, the unthinkable horrors of the Shoah and genocides known and unknown. Identity-as-wall has existed, and still exists, in all cultures, in all societies. But in the West, where it is amplified by science and technology, it has proven to be the most devastating. The world has nevertheless made Whole-World. Languages and cultures, civilizations, peoples have nevertheless encountered each another, collided with each another, embellished and enriched each another, often without knowing it or acknowledging it.

At an astonishing speed, the smallest invention, the smallest discovery, spreads throughout the world to all peoples, from the invention of the wheel to the practices of sedentary agriculture. Human progress cannot be conceived of without admitting that there is a dynamic side to identity, that of *Relation*. There, where identity-as-wall closes down, identity-as-relation opens up. And if, from the beginning, this side has permitted differences as well as opacities, this permission was never based on humanism or developed through the governing structure of a religious morality made secular. It was simply a matter of survival: those who survived the best, who reproduced the most successfully, were those who had known how to put this contact with the other into practice. They had known how to compensate for identity-as-wall with give-and-take and had known how to grow continuously in this way ... "I am able to change by exchanging with the Other, without, however, losing myself or becoming other than myself." It was therefore also an occasion for poetry, where *being-in-the-world* enlarges *being-in-itself*. Beauty is inseparable from the movement of the tides of humanity, from their indefatigable quest.

Identities are inevitably a part of this contact and exchange. It is the ineptitude of knowing how to live through this contact and exchange that creates the identitarian wall, which distorts identity. The final refusal of contact and exchange comes when we break the mirror so we can no longer see ourselves. To begin to refuse to see the other leads directly to a process of the self's contraction. The idea that one can "sustain" oneself and realize one's full potential can only be conceived of in the effervescence of contacts and exchanges, in connection with the other, with being in the world, and not in *a priori* or tenets that are policed.

On the back of faded glories, identity-as-wall was able to prop up those tribes, ethnicities, peoples, or nations that were confronted with nature's hostile ways, with the violence of all life, as it struggles doggedly for its own survival. For isolated or powerful groups, identity-as-wall was able to reaffirm itself through founding myths, national histories and vertical lineages (forming imperious genealogies). And yet, to the extent that the world opened itself to the presence of all, that even the most remote place in the world turned out to belong to the inescapable reality of the world at large (it was clear, for example, that abundance in one place was most often based upon lack somewhere else, that our misery could not abide by anyone else's happiness), it was the relational aspect of identity that appeared the most valid. Through it, we understand that nothing escapes the radiance of the Whole-World, which is neither confusion nor abandon. Walls and borders matter less when the world makes Whole-World, which amplifies the butterfly effect beyond what we can imagine.

Identity-as-wall can reassure people. It can serve the ends of racist, xenophobic, or populist politics to a consternating degree. But, stripped of every virtuous principle, the wall of identity no longer knows anything about the world. It protects nothing, opens up nothing, if not simply the spiral to regression, the insidious asphyxiation of the spirit and the loss of self.

The liberated imagination

The walls that are being constructed today (on the pretext of terrorism, uncontrolled immigration, or religious conflict) are not erected between civilizations, cultures or identities, but between forms of poverty and of superabundance, between opulent, restless intoxications and dry asphyxiations. Thus, they are erected between realities whose internal contradictions could be managed or mitigated – that is, resolved – by a global politics, provided with functional institutions.

The unyielding walls that rise against the miseries of the world curiously dissolve before the immigration of the rich, the emotional surges of finance, the hordes with their conquering merchandise, the tribes with their compulsory technologies and their services that standardize en masse and devour the unassuming in the wholly invisible voracity of economic liberalism. Suddenly submissive, these very walls seem to welcome these powers, which no longer flaunt national coats of arms, no longer claim a language, and arrive with their faces bared for all to see and yet are unknown, anonymous and uniform, encompassing all lands within their borders.

What threatens national identities is not immigration but other things: American hegemony, the insidious standardization of consumption, merchandise made into gods and thrust upon the innocents, the idea of a "Western essence" different from all others, or of a civilization entirely separate from all others, which by this token is no longer thought to be simply human. It is the idea of purity, of having been chosen, whether by God or not. It is the idea of pre-eminence, and the right to intervene. In short, it is the identitarian wall that determines the dynamics of human unity-in-diversity.

The catchphrase the "clash of civilizations" is to be lamented. Civilizations interact with each other, rub against each other, change and exchange both in conscious and unconscious ways, and have done so for thousands of years. Histories of culture – that is, of identities – find nothing but strata after strata dissolving into each other, nourishing each other, watching with each other, enriching each other, "emulsifying" each other. The "West" is in us, and we are in it. It is in us by way of suggestion, subjugation, and direct or silent domination. But it is also in us by way of these values that it holds so dear, and perhaps to excess (reason, individuality, human rights, gender equality, secularism, and citizenship), values that were already germinating to different degrees and with infinite nuances in all cultures. All cultures have magical-mythical imaginations linked to rational-technical processes. All cultures are equally wise and foolish, prosaic and poetic. All cultures are composed of communitarian impulses and individual action. Western domination was reinforced through a brutish extension and intensification of these givens: the worm was in the fruit. In creole, *sé kod yanm qui maré yanm*: it's the vine that gives birth to the yam that won't let go of the yam. Don't fall prey to your own devices.

Thus, all conquerors are secretly conquered. All those who dominate are ruined by nothing other than the alchemy of their domination. Taking over something opens up spaces to all sorts of secret influences. Those who exercise brutal and blind power are burdened by inescapable weaknesses. In taking over the world, the West was also taken over by it. At least in the hoped-for future, perhaps give-and-take will replace ritual pillaging.

The unique position of those defeated in the global market is that they received both the wonders and the shadows of those who have conquered them. What is difficult to do is not to reject them outright, but to undo their sterilizing fascinations through a liberated imagination, through the clairvoyant poetics of the Whole-World. An optimal fullness, far from conquests, from bitterness, from revenge or from thirst for domination, a fullness that is called worldliness. Now we are in the "West," but we are also orienting ourselves: we know our Orient.

Worldliness

Today, worldliness (which is not the same thing as the global market) invigorates us and wounds us. It suggests to us a type of diversity more complex than the type defined through the archaic markers of skin color, of the language we speak, of the god we worship or fear, and of the land where we were born. Relational identity opens up into a type of diversity that is a firework, an ovation of imaginations. The multiplicity, or the effervescence, of imaginations relies upon the vivifying, self-conscious presence of what all cultures, all people, all languages have brought to life in shadows and in wonders, which constitutes the infinite material life of all peoples. Real diversity is found today only in different conduits of the imagination: the manner of conceptualizing oneself, of conceptualizing the world, of conceptualizing oneself in the world, of organizing the principles of existence and of choosing one's native land. People of the same race can think about the world differently. The same way of thinking can be found in people with different skin colors, languages, and religions. Think of public figures known by all, Mrs Condoleezza Rice for example. She thinks about the world the same way as Mr George Bush does, which has close to nothing in common with how Mr Mandela or Martin Luther King may think of it. Likewise, a vague feeling of political or "racial" solidarity cannot serve as the basis to criticize those who work for Mr Nicolas Sarkozy and who, based upon their dark complexions, are evidently immigrants: they are more alike than not. "Sameness" is a chameleon. Diversity can just as easily confound identitarian clichés, disrupt things entirely and make it clear that discriminatory certitudes are no more than feeble prejudices.

The arts, literature, and music come together through a way of thinking that no longer respects national borders or arrogant languages, proud of their supposed distinctiveness. In worldliness (which is present today and yet remains for us to fully bring about), we do not belong to "homelands," to "nations," and certainly not to "domains," but to "places," to cascading languages, to liberated gods that might not demand to be worshipped, to native lands that we will have chosen, to languages that we will have desired: these geographies that we will have stitched together from things and visions. And these "places," having become inescapable (we can no longer turn our backs on them, but we also cannot circumscribe them within an irrevocable sign, or enclose them in walls) enter into relation with all places on earth. The luster of these places inaugurates the infinite insurrections of imaginations and welcomes this worldliness.

The risks of identities and their inevitability

These transformations of sensibility do not result in muddled confusion, and they do not provoke it.

Today we must vow to relinquish national identity. But not because the intensification of the idea of national identity produced endless injustices and denials of freedom in the historical interactions of peoples across the world. No collectivity, no community, whether privileged or oppressed, can renounce what it takes to be its national life, which has produced so many sumptuous exaltations of the spirit, so many inventions, and required so many sacrifices. But today we see that every collective identity is open, that it sustains itself only through its interactions with the world, and that it has a future only through this opening. The nation is no longer a stronghold. Its interest in the perspective of the Whole-World is no longer calculated solely through the short term. Today, national identity can no longer be thought of as arising from a single root. Such thinking would lead it to wither and die. But the nation that is open to expansion and to sharing reaffirms, by the same token, its non-hegemonic place in the world. It no longer roars but sings.

Relation-identities are open. But that does not mean they lack roots – merely that the root is no longer a stake, *an chouk*: it no longer kills everything around it but searches out (whether we want it to or not, whether we wall it in or not, or whether we try to contain it or not) other roots with which to share the nourishment of the earth. As there were nation-states, there will be relation-nations. As there were borders that separated and divided, there will be borders that distinguish and connect, and that distinguish only in order to connect. This augury does not ignore the terrible modern rivalries of nations, or the disasters perpetuated by wars waged out of self-interest, over religion, or over the acquisition of raw materials and fossil fuels – wars waged by empires or championed by religions. It only predicts that the time will come when the desire to dominate, to impose laws, to establish empires, when the pride of being the strongest and when the arrogance of controlling the truth will be considered the surest signs of barbarity at work in the history of humanity. Beyond its concern with its immediate social, political, economic or military survival, a great nation will henceforth know this to be true and grasp this change in the world.

Exchange often leads to change. But that does not mean that we will all drown in a whirlpool where identities lapse and collapse, where differences are effaced. Changing through exchange leads to enrichment in the truest sense of the word, and not a loss of self. This is true for an individual, as well as for a nation. A community that welcomes strangers, allows their differences – even their opacities – nevertheless does not lose its essence or risk dying out. On the contrary, it grows this way, it becomes more complete: with this new luster, a community burnishes what it is, what it has, as well as what it is becoming, and becomes that much more radiant. In all of human history, from the Gallo-Romans to the Brazilians, no social *métissage* has ever led to degeneration. Not a single instance of creolization has led to the utter effacement of any of its constitutive parts. There are so many presences in a drum circle, so many languages in a reggae song, or in a phrase from Faulkner, so many archipelagos in a jazz riff. And how many hearty laughs of freedom, of jubilation there will be when all of this converges!

There is so much diversity in the energy of this unity, which for us and with us steps into uncertainty, confronts the unforeseeable and incites the trembling of the world.

A community certainly has the right to "maintain its uniqueness," if this desire (or this fear) is present. But only on the condition that it does not regulate this "uniqueness" or put it into law. Identity is free to live and breathe only if it arises from the natural conditions of the collective whole, free of artificial constraints. It is just as impossible to imagine, for example, a Ministry of National Identity devoted to systematic *métissage*, or to pre-scribed mixing, as it is impossible to countenance this ministry charged with upholding the supposed integrity or the pretend transparency of national culture, ideas that only dictatorial regimes have actively attempted to codify. In fact, the interconnectedness of identities is tied to the interconnectivity of the world, which makes the richness of identity often hard to parse. We affirm our deeply held belief that identity is a mystery to live through, to live through expansively, to live through with the maximum openness. And that it is only by living out this mystery that we can say we live, that we know what it means to exist.

On repentance

Faced with this backwardness, we must address issues of economic equality and social possibility, as well as inventing, maintaining, and reassessing difficult debates about national politics. The incontrollable flux of immigration from poor to rich countries can be balanced by many measures that would not be disruptive, precipitous or irrevocable: the implementation of a deliberate and fair stabilization of the world economy; the taxation of international capital; the regulation of the biggest polluting countries; the re-establishment of raw-material revenues for countries of the Global South; the systematic transfer of technologies, everywhere that it is possible, in a manner that respects local cultures and customs; the patient, deliberate establishment of a network of North–South trade that is both lasting and fair; the pressing need for a written constitution of social progress that is valid everywhere and subject to opposition everywhere; and, for the worst cases of dispossession and hunger, the establishment of a right to citizenship, or multi-citizenship, valid everywhere and subject to opposition everywhere. These are some of the many utopias that it would be absurd to turn our backs on before trying. There is something in this that might give a soul to the International Monetary

Fund, the World Bank, and the World Trade Organization. There is something in this that might allow us to imagine new institutions that would truly see the world. In this, there is a set of great political principles for a rich and privileged country, which by publicly defending these principles, by studying them extensively then implementing them, would grow. All of us must learn to understand the depth of their caution, the radiance of their audacity and the height of their vision. But opening ourselves to these possibilities is incumbent upon us all.

Indeed, it would be mad to repeat the same old tune, to pretend to reverse or to stop the tides of immigration by a government decree. The tides of immigration follow the fault-lines of power in the world, the shocks and the ruptures of antagonistic alliances, the whims of social retrenchment, all the injustices of the day. In the word "immigration," there is life-giving breath. The most woebegone migrant can introduce differences, which are the best nourishment possible for identities. By contrast, "integration" is an arrogant tool that imperiously demands the immigrant to unconditionally surrender the self, leading to impoverishment. This is just like the phrase "to tolerate differences," which lords it over others and never abandons its sense of superiority. The phrase "co-development" is only a ruse to satisfy silent economic actors eyeing a quota system for deportations and eager to enjoy humiliating people at home. Co-development can only work through this simple truth: we are all in it together. It's an open boat – big enough for us all. No one will be saved alone. No society, no economy.

Each language sings one single melody in the concert of all languages. Each culture, each civilization, achieves its fullest expression by relating to others.

So it is not immigration that threatens or impoverishes, but the unyielding nature of walls and the fencing off of the self. This is why we have raised our voices: so that national histories will open up to the realities of the world; so that the vertical structure of national memories will become disordered through the sharing of memories; so that national pride can be nourished by the recognition of the shadows, as well as the lights, of its history. It is why we say again that repentance, about which we have heard so much talk, cannot be asked for or demanded. Moreover, we do not know who would ask for it: as for slavery, genocide, holocaust and colonization, it is important in each case to see history for what it is and to combine memories, not so some people will now hate themselves, but so history can be fully admitted, can be heard. The truest understanding of the world is never blissfully unaware, arrogant or closed; it is born from small tremors and then, from tremor to tremor, it rises into a clarifying return of consciousness. The idea of repentance tends to diminish the one who demands it, but it enlarges the one who can enact it. If we are incapable of daring to repent freely, beyond any moralizing or Christian sense of repentance, then a poverty of conscience must be feared.

The call

Walls threaten everyone, and from each side of their darkness. They sap the last life from what has been withering away on the side of deprivation. And they turn bitter what has been full of anguish on the other side, that of abundance. The relation to the other (in all of its forms, the animal, the vegetal, the cultural, and so the human) is, in our opinion, the highest, the most honorable, the most enriching part of us. Let the walls fall.

We ask that all the forces of humanity in Africa, Asia, Europe and the Americas, all dispossessed peoples, all "Republicans," all those who espouse "human rights," the inhabitants of the smallest countries, the island dwellers and archipelagic wanderers, as much as those who traipse from continent to continent, all artists, all men and women of knowledge and understanding, all organizations of brotherhood and goodwill, all those who make and who create, raise their voices, in every possible way, to protest against this ministry of walls that attempts to normalize us to the worst, habituate us little by little to the unbearable and lead us eventually to legitimize, silently and complicitly, the intolerable.

The opposite of beauty.

MSR

THE ADAMANT BEAUTY OF THE WORLD: TO BARACK OBAMA[1]

Édouard Glissant and Patrick Chamoiseau
January 2009

Rising from the Abyss

is the sound of centuries. The song of Ocean's valleys.

On the Atlantic Ocean floor sonorous seashells tangle with skulls, bones, and iron balls turned green. These depths hold the cemeteries of slave ships and of the many men who sailed them. Deeds of a greedy Western world, violated borders, flags raised and fallen. They dot a thick carpet woven of no one knows how many sons of Africa intended for the trade but never registered. There's no question that in every latitude many other open abysses have affected numberless people in the world both before and after the Slave Trade. But these transported Africans undid the separations of the world. They too opened up the Americas' vast spaces with violent bloodshed. They became a foundational part of the power of the United States, and at the same time one of its failures – a force and a flaw and the most valuable of vulnerabilities. They are within us. They are within you, Mr President.

They are all around, part of the intersecting histories of South American countries, Brazil and the Caribbean, in the archipelagic thinking now loosening continental thinking. Continents are imperious, have only one truth and they project themselves like an arrow. Archipelagos are fragile but available to the many truths of the present-day world. The ocean of the Slave Trade was thus a dark continent dragging in its train the Caribbean where plantations dependent on enslaved people were established.

---

[1] Text published for the first time by Éditions Galaade and the Institut du Tout-Monde in January 2009, on the occasion of Barack Obama's first election as president of the United States.

The remains of these ancestors shipped away to become the silt of the abysses, all those former worlds, were ground down until they truly became a new place. One world made Africa laminary. The Africas impregnated distant worlds. This fact makes it possible to see the Whole-World and to comprehend it – the Tout-Monde given to everyone, valid for everyone, multiple in its totality, based on the sonorous abysses. And now, because the nations of mankind recognize the United States of America as currently the one most dominant, this sound has come out of the depths through you, Mr President, to enthrall us. This reality, along with other realities, much that is bitter, much that is delicious, emerged from the Abyss as well, casting its growing shadow all around.

The first thing to say is that everybody in the world seems to have had the same idea about Barack Obama: that he would change both the very nature of life in the United States and the direction of its foreign policy (putting an end to the wars in Iraq and Afghanistan?), and as a result change the way the world would see this country, that he risked being assassinated, that he would be able to improve the condition of Blacks and other minorities, that he would contribute to a coming together of races, ethnicities, tribal alliances, that he would be able to improve the situation of poor people in his country and be effective in combatting the economic and banking crisis. Those are the most frequent, most obvious and commonplace opinions, repeated night and day, like mantras and articles of belief.

These opinions, prevailing before and during the election for the presidency of the United States, and continuing as equally strong convictions today (though perhaps the exercise of power will erode them), are unlikely to be abandoned because of the force of an unprecedented fact, which is that Barack Obama is an almost miraculous, but very much alive, result of a process that the various different public opinions and understandings of the world have refused to acknowledge up to this point: the creolization of modern societies as opposed to the traditional drives for exclusivity based on ethnicity, race, religion, and statism with which the world is currently familiar. The importance of this phenomenon is such that we thought we could and should initiate a public address to Barack Obama, because we think that he has really heard the cry of the world, the people's voice, the joyful or wounded song of countries.

Creolization: the silt that rose from the Abyss, shook everything up; mixed marriages, erratic mixtures, neuroses about purity, the whip and its opposite the cutlass, all together made something unpredictable and unstoppable. The unthinkable became a general principle. Dreaming a Whole-World. The most extreme and crazy violence turned this silt into a priceless experience. Always possible heights. Vertiginous depths. That excessiveness.

And every encounter in the world has its roots in this silt: your mother and your father experienced it in the possibility of their very improbable union. The Hawaiian mosaic and unforeseeable Indonesian period that followed in your childhood. And your wanderings across so many continents.

As they came into contact and exchanged with each other, the worlds gave rise to spaces where we must learn to exist. They were first born in the rolling sounds made by hidden seashells, conchs forever silenced and ancient skulls. From the outpourings of the abysses the Ocean created a stretch of archipelagos, not yet inhabited and secretly offering themselves to our imaginations. The reality of these archipelagos took hold in the surroundings. And now here you, son of the Abyss, who now offer unbroken hope for so many Americans and so many inhabitants of the Whole-World, people of every different sort, every shade of darkness – the discoverers of these new archipelagos.

The few times that Barack Obama has run for office are not evidence of Blacks seeking to take power, nor are they some disguised way of perpetuating white power from below, not some crude mixture of contradictory, never achieved intentions. They are, rather, the defence and illustration of the notion of diversity, which is not some ordinary inconsistency in the world but quite specifically its new force, making it so we don't stop being Black for the sole reason that we would be equally concerned about being white or red or yellow or multicolored, ad infinitum. This politics of diversity is also a poetics, generally considered to be the peak of the humanities, and it is one of the first things marking Mr Obama's presidential campaign. It is not surprising that it came to pass in the United States, not because this country is immensely powerful but because it is immensely self-contradictory. Diversity – agreed upon, not advertised, sometimes experienced as a tragic impossibility – is, nonetheless, one of the major advances of our times, because it authorizes and reinforces the encounter of difference, something that racists of every stripe are desperately afraid of. Both tendencies are present in that country.

Similarly, it isn't surprising that a Black (mixed with white but according to the criteria, the merest drop of black blood makes you Black in the United States) took this on, because the Black communities in most of the countries in the Americas to which they were deported, then oppressed and exploited, have consented (think of the Caribbean and Brazil), not only to interbreeding but to a creolization that has the power to cross racial barriers and is erratic, unpredictable, and always irresistible. In the United States, this unstoppable creolization predated mixed marriages, especially because the imprint of the enslavement of Blacks on mentalities and sensibilities was far stronger and more lasting there than anywhere else, making interbreeding inconceivable in general, and also because the hatred of (aversion to) mixing was possibly what characterized Protestant Puritanism in this new world in the first place. Barack Obama was unforeseeable in a country where any notion of getting together, any sort of togetherness or mixing, was vigorously rejected by a large part of the population, both Black and White. His victory – which is certainly theirs – is, however, not primarily a victory for Blacks but rather the victorious overcoming of the history of the United States by the United States themselves. The ambiguous and insurmountable idea presiding at the founding of the country was made clear and was surmounted not simply by the oppressed part of the nation but by the nation as a whole.

And this has raised the hopes not just of North Americans but of all Negroes on this planet, no matter what their race. They too are the sons of the Abyss, all the scattered abysses at the bottom of all the oceans or of all the devastated lands, populations that still bear those apparently ontological wounds recorded as open sores on their existence, their survival. They await you. They love you, they revere you, and they see you, alas, as living revenge for the tragedy of blackness and the endless other apocalypses and damnations of people. Revenge doesn't go very far, it makes up for nothing in the past; the only revenge worth living is one of overcoming barriers and freedom of the spirit.

A seashell, a conch touches a skull there, here the silt moves, releasing a bubble that rises from the depths of the Ocean not to scream, complain or hate, but simply entrusted with the darkest of darkness, peacefully to offer itself to the light.

Whether rising from actual slavery or oozing from endless damnations, the ontological wound, still bitter and fixed, makes the sound from the abysses inaudible, the dark silt text indecipherable, and yet that trembling wound carries the sound.

The bubble arising from the oblivion of the Abyss bursts on the surface of the world, like oxygen having forgotten none of the suffocation, like an open space ready to teach how deeply places have been stripped bare. It is not without meaning that someone our poetics considers a real son of the Abyss, is now achieving – in reality, in favor, and in poetics – great power in the nations of the world and will have the ability to influence the direction of the Whole-World.

In reality, and despite appearances, no one was surprised at the emergence of Barack Obama: the very fact that creolizations are unpredictable made it known in advance. But we have to go back to the time when observation, description, and theoretical research into such creolizing processes were conducted in the late 1980s. They demonstrated that, as in creole languages where syntaxes, lexicons, and ways of speaking come from sources completely foreign to each other, heterogeneous cultural elements coming together work at lightning speed with unexpected, unpredictable results and, although they don't remain intact, no element disappears or becomes distorted to the advantage of another. That doesn't mean that the population of the United States, perhaps with the exception of people from the Deep South, are creole in the same way that Caribbean people are. But jazz music, for example, is created on the basis of creolization, with its African substructure using Western instruments, which is how it became instantly valid for everyone. However, if we assume that cross-breeding is one of the main forms of creolization, we see that, up to this point, there has been very little mixing of races in the United States in comparison to the Caribbean or Brazil. The two groups identifying their origins as White and Black have remained separate from each other, like two unapproachable bodies. Moreover, other ethnic or national groups live side by side (referred to as multiculturalism) without much mixing.

In the United States, the oppression of Blacks was so savage and so cruel that it would be hard for the situation to be other than it is. Furthermore, particularly because of Protestant notions of purity, Whites have resisted racial mixing. But, despite this absence of any widespread or dramatic interbreeding, everybody sensed that American society tended strongly toward creolization, toward the mixing of cultures and the diversification of cultural phenomena (in that case, going far beyond multiculturalism), resulting in connections between different ethnic groups with a more and more unpredictable spread of combinations and mixes. This was not just one of the possibilities present in the evolution of this society; it was a probability. However, more than just a matter of elementary biology or cultural mixing, creolization is an unimaginable result of imaginations coming into contact.

The Negroes of the world, all of those in pain who expect that you will provide them with the distillate of an ultimate balm, are deluded. This expectation is part of their very weakness. The racism that people believe they are overcoming cannot be summarized by any logic. It often resists factual evidence and is unconvinced by any concrete proof that the opposite of what they believe is true – your existence would seem to be an elegant illustration of that opposite truth.

Nelson Mandela is, for example, one of the most admired men on the planet, as a symbol he is known far and wide; however, this has changed nothing about the beliefs of the world's racists, not just the really vicious ones – there are also insidious, hypocritical racists. As regards international celebrities, Black or famous mixed-race people, movie stars, renowned musicians, major international officials, ministers and secretaries of state, governors of federations, sports gods, they are admired just as much by racists of the most obvious sort as by anyone else (one might call this the gladiator syndrome, or mercenary logic where individuals are both adulated and reviled) and have had no effect on sick minds. One Black man with the greatest possible power at his disposal (a priceless symbol) will not magically change the immediate condition of Blacks in the United States or in the world, nor will his election change the immediate condition of people subjected to capitalist rule and western standards. In the case of Mandela, as in your own, the symbol is nonetheless uplifting, vital, not because it can directly change things, but because it allows us to make the strongest possible case about everything sick and unbearable about relations among human beings whenever they are lumped together into collective bodies.

Political society in the United States was behind in terms of reality, because traditionally control of it was confiscated by White hands. Blacks weren't able to get into the game except very slowly and on the local level, in certain cities and particular institutions in the various states, because of the hegemony of elite Whites who had managed to organize themselves into political dynasties and large, dominant families. But Obama escapes this dichotomy because he isn't exactly a Black in the United States, he's not "African-American." His father is an African – not a descendent of slaves from Texas or Georgia. Therefore, he comes directly from the place that is a dream and a hope for many African-Americans, the place to which they want to return. Even so, he is well acquainted with the Abyss and knows it all the better. When Obama emerged as a political phenomenon in the United States, a majority of Blacks were not in favor of him. They perhaps tended to think of him as "not Black enough." And, in the same way, a majority of Whites were "not for him" because they considered him completely Black. That Barack Obama was able to overcome these obstacles, this impossibility, means American political life has finally and with great difficulty begun to catch up with the reality of the social and ethnic composition of this nation on the move. Despite the Kill Obama signs already popping up. After making this initial journey, Obama, the candidate for senator, disappeared and then Barack Obama was born. With him multiplicity entered the political consciousness of the country, after having made its mark on the population, social composition and its convulsions.

The immigration of Latin-Americans, Central and Eastern Europeans, Koreans and other Asians must be taken into account. This flow of migrants disrupted the traditional head-to-head relationship between Whites and Blacks, almost all of the Indians having been massacred or neutralized right from the start. Arguably, they are likely to come back to life, rising up from the Abyss. Because what remains admirable about creolization is that it doesn't let its components disappear but rather helps them to recreate themselves. This other form of association, the unexpected mix, gives American society a new dimension as well as providing its reactions and tendencies with an unprecedented meaning. Moreover, it was interesting during the debate between Barack Obama and his various competitors to see how the adversaries competed for the votes of Chicanos, Asians or Jews, and just as telling to see that, counter to all expectations, Barack Obama won a large majority of those votes.

For a long time, everyone in the country predicted that "this" would happen. The intellectual class was perhaps behind the times because it was still talking about multiculturalism, melting-pot, hybridization – all of these were ways of limiting, in fact, knowledge of the incipient movement toward complete creolization and maintaining the head-to-head relationship between Blacks and Whites – to the detriment of the former. But the emergence of Barack Obama will not be without difficulties. The more his strategies move forward in the direction of a Poetics of Relation, as expressed magnificently in the overall direction of his electoral campaign, to then be signed by a victory that so far has transcended politics, the more the purulent, virulent racism will increase in the United States. An antibody to this virus is the increasing complexity of the society, its inextricable entanglements, fueled by influxes of immigrants, and in the end its recognition of this inextricability.

Repetitions: "Walls threaten everybody, on both sides, by the shadow they cast. They finish drying everything that has already run dry in one side's destitution, and completely sour the other side with anxiety over its abundance." There are so many walkways and bridges to build with the materials from these walls overturned even as they were being put up.

What is a Poetics of Relation that is mainly put in practice in the political arena? It seems, Sir, that you have given us the answer. First, once notions of distribution, exchange, and mixing are transformed in the collective imagination, it is the will never to turn back out of laziness or fear of the unforeseen. It is the determination to find other solutions, uncontrolled if need be, often surprising, when former models want to impose their framework or shackles permanently in a way that is sterile. It is stubbornly refusing to impose anything, whether spiritual, intellectual or material, through force, especially those ideas that one is absolutely certain are the most wonderful. And, whenever the long-standing forums of old assemblies abundantly demonstrate their uselessness, it is the pleasure of seeking and finding other venues for meeting and discussion. Indeed, we are saying that these reflexes, created by poetics, are political and they establish a politics. The increasing complexity of social entities throughout the countries of the world authorize the decisions, exchanges, and changes that arise with every shift.

The vertigo caused by complexity

As Barack Obama's main opponent said: "*He* is not like us." That "us" is entirely WASP – White Anglo-Saxon Protestant – it only knows the simplistic division of White and Black. What she doesn't know is that, when she says that, she herself is not "like" a large portion of the people of the United States – Whites, Blacks, or those from all sorts of places – and in any case, that she is distancing herself from who they are becoming: "She isn't reading the world and the world isn't read through her." It is likely that the society of the United States will get past this stumbling block of racist division (the alternative being an accepted, if not official, fascism), but surely not without losses and tragedies. It is possible that, where this election is concerned, no matter what its immediate results and those to come long after, violent oppositions among ethnic groups will occur. It seems that, even if Barack Obama's government ends up moving to the right, whether through a natural tendency or a strategic choice, it will not put an end to these upheavals. In any case, the present trend can never be undone: something is operating that has escaped from the Abyss or been fed by the earth. Everyone considers Barack Obama to be a brilliant illustration, complete and absolute, of the phenomenon of creolization, which people are becoming more and more conscious of, with all the tragedies and all the subtleties that the new situation will unleash. The emergence of this leader means that the world of the United States has truly become an American world – that is, it is new in its genuine multiplicity. The population of the United States is finally, symbolically and very concretely, a people of the Americas, among the other Americans.

Cuba, barrier free – now!

Haiti, in a state of total emergency – counter the intolerable, the abhorrent, immediately!

The residents of the United States expected this, although they didn't know or didn't dare know it. Obama is a solution to ethnic, racial, and social impossibilities. The first impossibility is that no one says the men who wrote the Constitution, the Founding Fathers, the country's almost mythical heroes, rightfully celebrated and honored – Jefferson and Washington – both owned slaves. On his deathbed, Jefferson, the man who wrote the magnificent words "all men are created equal," refused to free his slaves – probably so his heirs wouldn't be financially ruined. Unspoken words like those are impossible for a community. Unless we agree with the idea that a Black is not really a man. Obama makes up for American history: he compensates for what is unspoken; he closes a different sort of abyss. It is rather interesting to observe that when he refers to the Founding Fathers he does so plainly, wholeheartedly, and without reservation. And on this occasion he apparently set aside the general situation of Blacks and other minorities in the country in favor of the Union (a unity) which was what Abraham Lincoln had earlier put first. Unless he was aware of bringing Blacks and other minorities into this Union at that very moment, bringing them in their own right, fully and for the first time into the history of the country.

African-Americans didn't acknowledge you at first. They were unable to come to grips with this complexity. Sons of the Abyss, still marked by the initial pain of the silt of the pit of the Atlantic and the mud of Plantations, they remained suffering repositories that refused to be erased. They have almost always wanted to leap over the Atlantic Abyss to contact and return to Africa, to find there some certitude and even give the afflicted dream of Liberia and Sierra Leone a try, those places in a dead-end struggle over ancestral territories. Elevating Africa to the level of a fantasmatic paradigm, they fix it there, immobilizing themselves symbolically in it. Who could reproach them for that or lecture them on the subject?

Sons of the Abyss, they no longer belong to those ancient worlds but often they ignore that. And often, unknowingly, they are Yankees (full of a kind of supremacy), and consequently completely lacking in caution. The urgency of their struggle, the intense confrontations, the enormous number of daily injustices that they must not give in to only rarely make possible the beginnings of a path toward the new part of the world with its archipelagos. Meaning toward themselves in all their diversity. When one says "African-American," it is as if an African essence has been plugged into America. A precious armor but the opposite of being alive. What you are says that, and the way people listen to you says it too.

If they come together in you, in this vertigo, in the audiences of silt risen out of the Abyss and in the unfathomable complexities of the Tout-Monde, the Whole World, it is because they now have a thousand chances to transform their adhesion into an open, inclusive energy that can only benefit the United States. Their movement toward you, with you, as part of the whole population of the United States will also be priceless for every consciousness developing in the Tout-Monde. The slightest movement toward complexity – a song, a poem, the quivering of a people – immensely enhances the whole, creating connection with the smallest detail. Consciousness extends. Imagination expands. Then this Whole-World consciousness demands expression or acknowledgement, politically and poetically.

A dormant, suffering energy comes awake to this complexity, and has no fear of becoming lost or distorted. And being as you are, a son of the Abyss and Tout-Monde's vertigo, you will perhaps set in motion struggles still stuck in the shackles of the old imagination all over the planet. Basing everyone's hope where the world's connections are most afflicted!

Repetitions: "The incontrollable flux of immigration from poor to rich countries can be balanced by many measures that would not be disruptive, precipitous, or irrevocable." These measures would derive from a Poetic of Relation.

Barack Obama's famous speech on race really dealt with the relations between races and, subtly, between social classes. The speech demonstrated his great knowledge of the situation, but also his great ability to find new strategies for approaching the problem. The usual ways these problems of race are treated are, perhaps, inadequate because they don't make it possible to go beyond particular situations. We think, for example, about the Black minister who was full of reproaches for Barack Obama. We can see what he was quite correctly getting at: when we look back on the history of American Blacks, what they so long endured in forced labor, humiliations, ignorance, less than basic living conditions, epidemics, tortures, lynchings, segregation with no recourse, both before and after the Civil War, it is normal to find it hard to admit that one can accommodate solutions. But, obviously, the minister's way of doing things is not the most effective one now, nor the most just; moreover, it is not the one that will be the most productive. He came close to putting Obama in an impossible situation. Doubtless he too wept on the celebrated night of that victory as the oxygen relieved him of his virtuous suffocation. Let's hope he shook hands with Barack Obama.

The same blind approaches are found among a great many Whites, but there the only motivation is a passion for racial domination. The woman we will call The Objector, come from the land of ice, is totally blind: she knows nothing of the reality of her country. Her Alaska might as well be right next door to the little towns of the Deep South where the Ku Klux Klan thrives. It is a terrifying aspect of American civil society. It is not worth going into details, but such an attitude is monstrous. It is perhaps the side of the United States that will take the longest to go away. At the same time, trends move so quickly in that society, its size speeds up the impact when all the particles and all the originally separate parts of the collectivity meet, and today's reality is that the new president is indeed a Black, according to the very criteria established in that country. Immigration seems more and more to dominate racial specificities. The inflow of immigrants and the speed with which they fit into society prevent any entirely pessimistic predictions on the subject.

Everything said about the Black struggle, before and after the Civil War, and since the 1960s, is more timely than ever. Without Rosa Parks and Martin Luther King, without the murdered Black Panthers, without the unflagging marches, without the riots in the big cities, without the scandal of young Blacks beaten in the streets by the police, without Muhammed Ali and Malcolm X, Obama would not have been possible. But these struggles in the name of the right for Blacks to exist also confined their action to simply opposing the thought and reality of White supremacy, a still-current ideology. It was absolutely necessary to steadfastly maintain that opposition. Obama, however, quite logically goes beyond this framework. He brings all the minorities together – in other words, *he isn't asking anything of Whites as such nor is he requiring anything of them* (a great many of them followed him, were inspired by him, wept with the Blacks at the thrilling moment of victory, and now he can put his own decisions into action); on the contrary, he has a lot to offer them, specifically a real occasion to participate in the rise of a great country of mixing and equality – that is his brilliant victory. Creolization is a tumultuous fusion with surprising results.

These scraps of truths, these remnants of certainties, the first unit's debris from its collapse when struck by the great crime, truths embarked in the currents of the deep and swept along by the breath of the same winds that drove the slave ships, now can be seen in these mixing – the collisions, alliances, illusions, chaos, blindings and seeings, former fixations, daring visions, motionless wanderings – this great tumultuous parade to the Whole-World: all of that is Relation.

Possibilities, the burning imaginations, whose sense or senselessness we must live with, are found in Relation.

If we ignore Relation, we are subject to it, we go about it as sub-relations. If we think it and live it and act it out, we impart to it the bursts of imagination, the brilliant light of poetics, the visions of politics, we force it into beauty. Exploitation, crime, and domination are never open to sensing beauty.

There is no beauty in the briefs of loners, fundamentalisms, unshared national Histories, ethnic purges, negation of the other, expulsion of immigrants, sealed-off *certainty. No more beauty in the essentialism of race or identity. No beauty in the capitalizing of production, financial hysteria, the craziness of markets or over-consumption.*

The deficit of beauty is the sign of life being violated. It calls for resistance. In contact with beauty, resistance, existence and politics get a deep charge of life. René Char: "There is no one place in our darkness for beauty. The whole place belongs to beauty."

Aimé Césaire: "Justice listens at the doors of beauty." Is there now beauty in remembering together, we who have come from every direction? Or on the contrary, must we simply require repayment, insist on the debt, impose life interest?

The one who grants reparations for the damage of slavery makes himself look big, and the one demanding or insisting upon it lowers himself. Black Africa is the one exception to that. The Africa that was globally rejected, permanently thrown by the slave trade into fathomless depths of poverty and under-development. In that regard, Western countries owe a debt to Africa. This original debt must be paid. It would not be an act of charity or reparation. We also believe that relentlessly demanding redress (or even repentance) would prevent thinking or doing anything else. Had Obama devoted his political activity and powers full time to demanding such reparations, he would probably not have had either the opportunity or the energy to work on solidifying his prospects of being elected president of the United States, and then go on to have a successful term of office, which is already and probably will be one of the greatest steps of progress taken for everybody in the world and for the Whole-World. And now will he demand reparations from himself? No, he will enact justice for the less fortunate of his country and on behalf of countries just starting up and those brought low – that is our hope.

Designate Black Africans as central to every urgent situation in the Whole-World. Remember the crimes suffered, teach histories about the lack of balance in their perspectives, repair the damage done, cancel debts, open access to training and knowledge, establish fair practices in everything, enact laws everywhere against predatory practices – Call them out!

Create an international court of law to decide economic and financial crimes, because riots caused by hunger, haggard emigrations, disasters which wipe out populations are never a matter of spontaneous generation. There should be no zones of impunity nor unidentified crimes in the Whole-World – Get started!

Through a worldwide authority, distribute among places of abundance, according to the quantity they hold of the planet's riches, the portion of immigration they are to absorb, the burdens of poverty they are to assume, their duties in the face of the flood of catastrophes confronting us, so they all quench all these thirsts, feed these famine – Dare!

The cry of the world

Nowadays in France, as in many other favored countries, everybody needs to show they have a Black: administrations display their officers, televisions fill the stages and seats of their news hours with these suddenly precious (for the time being) specimens, and no doubt soon the political parties will display banners dark with "diversity." Skills that were formerly invisible will have opportunities – that's a good thing – and those who are mediocre will be in a tizzy, holding their breath so as to benefit. As far as we're concerned, anyone who has to have a Black man become president of the United States in order to grant Blacks the virtue of humanity is the lowest of the low. We don't have to stand up to racist views with anti-racism or some model of virtuous racialization; we make them invalid by our immediate and peaceful use of a different way of imagining whose starting point is the pure sparkle of differences, the shocks and oppositions of those differences and the alliances they make as a starting point.

Repetitions: "I am able to change by exchanging with the Other, without, however, losing myself or becoming other than myself."

You are a result of Relation, but it is possible that your way of thinking, your imagination, did not take shape there. It is also the product of your history and your consciousness as a citizen of the United States within the Whole-World. That is why it is vital for the sound of the Abyss in the distance to be widely heard, for the old fixed ways to be abandoned and for everyone to be able to experience the song from the Abyss, learn from it, draw power from it, and for the worlds to create the Whole-World. You are open to the miseries of the world, sensitive to its poverty, its opacities. We beg of you, don't lose any part of the profound song from the Abyss. Make it into a politics where the Whole-World seeks itself as much as it finds itself, invents itself as much as it imagines itself. Go out into the Whole-World the way a young poet goes! That, perhaps, is the most realistic form of politics.

But we're not sure that President Barack Obama will escape the fatal circle determined by imperialism. He is, of course, more capable than others of doing this, because the transformations at the heart of American society can carry him along. But the people of the United States sincerely believe it is their calling to run the world. This applies both to the people who side with capitalists wishing to monopolize oil and its wealth and to those on Obama's side who want to try to fix things – implying that they will make them better. This feeling comes from their impression of having surpassed Europe, where they came from, and their sense of being so far ahead of the rest of the world. An African or a Korean or a Scot who has become a citizen of the United States can believe, from that point on, that they are above the rest of the world. This will to run things is all the more troubling because most of those who believe it deepest are generally ignorant of that world, or have forgotten it. Before invading Iraq, they didn't know that it was a region that was heir to a great civilization more than 3,000 years old. Specialists were the only ones able to foresee and then organize the pillage of the museums of Baghdad. The world's relations with the United States are complicated and usually based on relative force. Barack Obama has been elected president, and what is important is not at all that the world better appreciates that country. The important thing is for the United States to better appreciate the world. What is at stake in Obama's election is, for example, for the whole country to know that an Iraqi is not a savage. The hope is that, as with other effects or other results of every process of creolization, not only does Barack Obama seem to know the world, but he also seems to have a proper sense of it.

Will this "poetics," which is also a miracle and has been able to create a politics, be able to survive this exhilarating time – this electoral campaign and the victory concluding it – and go on to resist the obligations implicit in the new chief of foreign affairs and armed forces of such a country? Utopia is what is lacking in this world and the only realism able to untangle the knot of impossibilities. What a worldwide and invisible system can fear is not that you are a Black man (it will make accommodations and keep on making profits), but that you are part of some force unknown to its hounds and its inevitabilities, and that this force might invent its own path.

The formulaic misunderstanding US citizens have of the world is a continuation of the practice of continental conquest in the tradition of the Far West. Essentially, we think the mental, spiritual, and social equilibrium of the United States has been based primarily on this experience of the Far West, including the fall-out in racist views, speedy justice, the right to bear arms, the untold story of the life and death of the Indians, sheriffs, lynchings, the reflexive law of an eye for an eye, the destruction of landscapes and massacre of wild animals – the buffalo and bears, and so on. It was a matter of creating the union of the United States throughout the continent as quickly as possible, and this was then the world – really the world – for those pioneers and their constituencies in the eastern part of the country. Savage violence, the quickest path to that union, settled into the big cities as well, and scarred the Civil War. Then the armed forces were delegated the task of continuing it, expanding into the world (toward Mexico, the Pacific next, then Japan and China). The citizens of the United States, however, had no interest in the world; what impassioned them was to "realize" the North American continent. They almost didn't enter the two World Wars. The domination by the United States is, moreover, not essentially territorial: it is financial, economic, and strategic everywhere. It is not an imperialism of spatial conquest. It is not based on populating colonies, precisely because the country had been a colony itself and mistrusted that situation. It was content with occupying strategic parts of the globe and, rather than trailblazing pioneers in the model set by the Far West, the tenants who are more like, for example, the ruthless representatives of United Fruit in South America. It is very significant that the separate regions of the United States, Alaska, Puerto Rico and Hawaii, are almost specks of dust (both in space occupied and in significance) in relation to the continental subset.

This is because the politics and thought of the United States were above all strongly and rigidly continental in nature (as straightforward as a rush to the West and based on systems that were, in general, without nuance – "It's against the law" – projecting bluntly outward, an arrow-like projection, and sacrificing everything to the idea that the country had created itself and did so all by itself, with no need for anyone else). However, a problem has come up. Perhaps this continent, which was apparently created as a bloc or strove fiercely to become one, is now archipeligizing. To become an archipelago does not consist of fracturing, nor does it result in weakness. But it does reject ready-made ideas.

So now the country is catching up with its astonishing diversity, no longer to create a monolithic unit, but rather to live its astounding, contradictory, teeming differences, in the long echoes of the Abyss and the sound of the Whole-World. It is there, rather than the coast of California, that the Far-West becomes complete, or actually becomes transformed.

In relation, force is not power

Sir, the question, one which is perhaps impertinent, would be to ask whether you are a Yankee – one whose nature is to govern, although probably less arrogantly and less blindly than most of your political adversaries or predecessors.

Because the people of the United States think that their country was given, or assumed for itself, the mission of running the world. However, once beyond the tragic dominations, peoples have no aim other than that of entering into Relation, to become richer through sharing, creating themselves only through exchange.

Because you believe in the effectiveness, or perhaps convenience, of force. However, in the unfathomable labyrinths of the Whole-World, force that always believes only in itself always has never found anything but limitations: weaknesses and powerlessness both in the Korean War and in Afghanistan.

Military force as well as financial, economic force. Everyone in the world, assessing this force, has the arrogance to believe that they can overwhelm you with advice and warnings, but this is because hope and anxiety are at play there: you have caused us to give some thought to what the United States proposes or imposes on the world. It thus seems that your election, paradoxically, may have reinforced your country's influence in the world. From now on, the world's opinions when it thinks about you will move in sharply opposing directions: (nothing will change), (everything is now possible).

Thus, therefore, it would take daring to imagine the dollar no longer the only standard international currency – which would be the first step toward getting the United States out of the delicate position of being the one designated responsible for the fortunes or crises of the international financial system. De Gaulle sensed this and wanted gold, rather than the dollar, to be the standard currency. As long as the dollar is the standard currency, the United States doesn't care about having $10,000 billion of debt. Tax havens, one of the great causes of international economic disorder, are places where you can pile up dollars, or their banking equivalents, but you can't do this with gold. It is the United States that is expected to do whatever might slow down or calm international economic disorder. Pledges and orders made by US officials and policy-makers determine market rates throughout the world, and influence financial actions and commodity prices. Only raw materials, petroleum and strategic metals are regulated by directorates that no one knows anything about.

But today the United States seems overwhelmed, caught up in its own torment. They need to imagine solutions and perhaps capitalist realism will no longer suffice. They have to accept that, for these solutions, everyone has to be part of the decision making. In the absence of such radical measures (because who could "replace" the dollar?), perhaps we will have to anticipate seeing what other sorts of new steps you imagine can be taken, outside of or alongside the constraints of routine economic and political requirements (and frameworks). Because in the present crisis there were no distortions or perversions but rather the revelation of an intrinsic absurdity. We must beware of the possibility that the system has the potential to challenge itself and even become stronger through this challenge.

The well-known cultural dominance of the United States, moreover, seems to be both real and imaginary. In the first place, the hegemony of Anglo-American culture can only happen by neglecting the English language. Anglo-American is a language where 500 or 1000 spoken words can manage international relations, commerce, scientific techniques, sporting events, performing arts, and publishing successes when translations of foreign works are appropriately formatted. A language, however, is a living body; it moves forward, it figures things out, it has areas of darkness and hesitation. We don't believe that shackling the living Tout-Monde, where unpredictability is the main source of energy, to a dominant language that is powerful in scope and structurally weak is an option.

We believe in the future of little countries, places that escape the ruthless, globalizing logic that thrives on innovations, on what speculators call quick fixes. We believe in divining the infinite number of possibilities not yet dreamt of.

We believe that in the churning, multiple world toward which we are moving, languages will multiply their potentials for existence and relation – meaning their implicit resistance to homogeneity, even if they resist through means that are obscure and unknown. They will "comprehend" each other, which implies that they will maintain no ontological barriers between each other.

It seems to us that official theatre and film of the United States, and indeed its arts (with their overwhelming resources), have taken – perhaps even stretched – the art of beauty, considered as the synonym and model of efficiency, to its limit in terms of its influence on sensibilities scattered throughout the worlds, but that perhaps they have become, little by little and more and more, past history compared with a lively, quivering approach to beauty, where beauty, more often than not, is some awesome figment.

And we foresee that the imposition of US ways of life may not resist a worldwide economic crisis. This is our vision for all this complexity, which perhaps will also occasion the blossoming of countless explosive creativities in this country where all is open and everything is possible.

Only diversity triumphs over empires. But diversity also saves, enhances, and multiplies the vital elements of every empire that exists and henceforth functions outside of those self-imposed, imperial laws. The world needs the dynamic energies of Relation (of change) that are everywhere active, beyond deadly competition and the appetite for profit. In the United States, as in China or India, Brazil or the Polynesian archipelagos, Mexico or in no matter what isolated mountain village, somewhere in the wide world. Thus a worldwide politics needs a forum that is constantly central to an audience of everyone, nurtured by everyone and concerned about everyone. An organized intensity.

Today, people everywhere have a sense that the force nations have is not what makes them great anymore. Nor is it the belief these nations have in their values alone that does so, because no people possesses the complete truth of human conditions and no people is unique – all peoples are unique and no one of them is so entirely. The greatness of a nation arises from the justice of its intuitions when it is a matter of relations among all nations and all communities, and this greatness is confirmed by the measures this nation might propose or take in order to bring these relations into balance. It is not at all important that these proposals may be mocked as utopian and kept in the margins of the harshest realities; they nonetheless forge a path in the imagination of the human race. Utopia is always the path we miss.

Repetitions: "The walls that are being constructed today (on the pretext of terrorism, uncontrolled immigration, or religious conflict) are not erected between civilizations, cultures or identities, but between forms of poverty and of superabundance, between opulent, restless intoxications and dry asphyxiations. Thus, they are erected between realities whose internal contradictions could be managed or mitigated, that is, resolved, by a global politics, provided with functional institutions.

The unyielding walls that rise against the miseries of the world curiously dissolve in front of the immigration of the rich, the emotional surges of finance, the hordes with their conquering merchandise, the tribes with their compulsory technologies and their services that standardize en masse and that devour the unassuming in the wholly invisible voracity of economic liberalism. Suddenly submissive, these very walls seem to welcome these powers, which no longer flaunt national coats of arms, no longer claim a language, and arrive with their faces bared for all to see and yet are unknown, anonymous and uniform, encompassing all lands within their borders."

We don't recognize these forces anywhere. Because they have no real place.

In the same way, we see the universe of technical knowledge, with the United States its most efficient conductor, as an opaque body of unpredictable discoveries and, at the same time, a world that is fixed and divided. In the European Middle Ages, the artisans or artists who reproduced the manuscripts (the monks who were the copyists) perhaps viewed the birth of the printing press as a barbarity that would destroy the stylistic, textual, and calligraphic quality of the beautiful original manuscripts. We should not accede to elitist reactions against anything. Are texts or chats going to create a new style? Possibly. Are they going to sterilize any of style's possibilities – that is, any new connivance between language and ideas? Possibly. We shouldn't form a premature or fixed opinion on such questions. But we have to leave them alone and let them be. The *Poetics of Relation* is unforeseeable, unpredictable. It as easily includes the most remote traditions of the past, even the most distant past, which suddenly are able to be revived, along with the most daring technologies of the future, which gradually can regress to being silent relics. Let's give the same thought and attention to a crazy metropolis that takes up all the air around it and an island no higher than the green sea surrounding it, and seemingly extinguished in a forgotten sea.

The Whole-World is sensitive to the warmth of utopia, the oxygen of a dream, the beautiful errantry of a poetics. It appoints art, and what art can divine, to rule over our global politics and the words we share. It even brings us to where we can foresee this new region of the world, which we are entering all together, through so many different ways and actions.

An infinity of archipelagos that we must inhabit, not strings of islands (common markets or strategic alliances, capitalists' vacation homes or schools of financial fingerlings), but places connected by a thousand shores, not needing codes to know each other, moving beyond things formerly impossible. Imaginations that drift and intersect across oceans, beyond borders, in the silence or turmoil of the gods, throughout continents, in the sprinkled island-seeds, raising a geography that nobody could draw because it is instantly gone.

In the Whole-World's fathomless repercussions, every injustice becomes a whirlwind feeding hurricanes and endlessly reviving smoldering embers. We can see this in the inextinguishable Palestinian war. Jerusalem, the homeland for all peoples, is establishing a space open to two guardian states! Right now.

Nelson Mandela, throughout 28 years of a solitude that was, we would like to believe, shared with everyone, thought about his country, and about his country in the Whole-World; he thought and acted in the broadest manner possible, and he quickly became distanced from power. He left Power to become powerful.

Justice in Palestine, not through Power, through force, but in the power of what is right. Justice in Israel, not through Power, but through the power of fairly sharing. Justice in every forsaken place, left to massacres, pandemics, or simply abandoned to the mercy of water, wind, and fire.

Countries and cities that are meeting places, places of sharing, symbiosis or simply coexistence, as in Sarajevo and Beirut – or creole like New Orleans and Port-au-Prince – are systematically considered targets by fundamentalists from everywhere, or unremittingly subjected to unmentionable poverty or abandoned to their fate when the worst catastrophes strike. With regard to the abandonment of the inhabitants of New Orleans after Hurricane Katrina, we can see that that was not a unique case: each time that powerless peoples are left to nature's blows, it usually takes unbearably long for help to come. This is the result of a right that rich countries have proclaimed for themselves: the right of interference. They intervene when and where they want and in their own good time. But New Orleans is part of a rich, developed country. It is just that this strangely captivating city is deemed to be "Black" and creole, hence unimportant. On this occasion, neglect by the federal government offended even its most faithful partisans. The Black part of the population considered it to be characteristically racist. But they weren't the only ones. It must repeatedly be said that *New Orleans is, like many others, a creole city: its diversity doesn't particularly desire to seem that way nor is this a matter of pride for it.* A city of creolization. We mustn't allow them to let cities of creolization die. Jeff Humphries, a white poet who lived there for a while, spent two weeks living through the post-hurricane disaster. He wrote an account of this shared suffering in a book entitled *Katrina, mon amour.* He didn't speak for himself but rather for an entire cosmos of ethnicities and people who were all in it together, with no other connection than the city itself.

These days all our cities, all our countries are in a state of diagenesis, its origins wild and widespread. Diagenesis is an occurrence opening up to a thousand possibilities in the past, the present, and the future. The thousand possibilities of this metamorphosis preserve us from doctrine and dogma, and move us into the regeneration that is available in what is uncertain, unforeseeable, and unpredictable.

The mysterious principle that animates life provides every existence with an irreducible uniqueness, but also an opacity that is approachable. Whence the infinite diversity, and the things that are unforeseeable in each existence, as well as the necessity of preserving them, their unpredictability as well as their opacity.

Tout-Monde, Whole-World is a field of unstable forces where the effervescence of a single imagination is able to produce waves that will have a determining effect at a distance. The Ocean's abyss was our opening to Relation.

You who have brothers and cousins and nephews and family friends on every continent, listen to what Relation is saying. There is a shimmer of linked Places now outlining non-state states in the Whole-World. Think in "places": sketch out the world's new region.

We know that our places are essential. We can't surround them with walls and forbid the other to enter, but we can exchange them without losing them, walk from San Francisco to Carthagena de Indias, and from rural Trinidad to the fjords – those wounds on Scandinavian shores. We can have a pleasant stopover in Iceland and spend a long time reading the sagas or listen to the griot's tales on the streets of Bamako. We don't come to conquer or colonize – this is no brazen invasion, we are playing tourist, the better to paint the insides of countries and the sky's abysses. And when places are forbidden to us, because the people in charge there are racist, intolerant, proud and arrogant in equal parts, as well as professionals at expulsion, we can turn those places around in our imaginations and sing them, thus changing them at a distance. We are able to sing with them, with the people claiming to be the sole owners who, according to the philosophy of Native Americans, should only consider themselves as its guardians. If we want to save the Earth, we have to stop taking it to be an object that is ours.

Everyone will encounter in Relation his or her places, languages, musics, texts, sometimes his or her teacher, brothers and cousins, a father and a mother, plenty of companions in errantry, twins in poetics and comrades through rhizomatic roots. We'll choose the land of our birth, and choose our gods without perhaps adoring them, we'll invent peoples and tongues, as intense as they come in that wandering that gives us direction.

This world that is bound together through its infinite number of possibilities and impossibilities, harmonies and disharmonies, reproductive ruptures and cohesive contrasts opens this other region where we have to learn to figure things out in order to move forward. It is a region we have never lacked; it was inside us and we were inside it, but somehow we missed seeing it.

Everything has changed, secretly and unquantifiably. We need something better than knowledge there; we need a poetics of what is continually happening around us. The power of a man or a nation can only be measured by their capacity to be in relation to the Places of the world, generating the richness and diversities there to create from them the best way to share them. Power exists in the brilliance of connection, in whatever connects, joins, reconnects, relays these things that are possible, these individuals and worlds.

The Power of the United States would have to be transformed, or at least be commuted into power, through a horizontal perception of its emergence in an emerging world. Your singular equation, Sir, offers a chance at this other beautiful utopia. Power only exists in Relation and this power is everyone's.

Every politics will thus be evaluated by its intensity in Relation. And there are more paths and horizons in tremors and fragility than in all-powerfulness.

Relation identity fills the space and thought of the archipelago. It doesn't kill what's around it as a single root-identity does; it weaves its joint and several roots, which go out to meet each other and mutually reinforce each other. This is what all the American spaces will do once we are done with these murderous times. The spaces of the world, once they have been cleared of the miasmas of the thought of uniqueness. All the continents, once they have been diverted into fragile, united archipelagos.

The horizontal wholeness of life. We see an inexorable parallel between social and ecologic collapse, the same predation accelerates them. The same attitude combats them. Let the poles, the remaining pack ice, the dried up countryside live, reforest the stripped hillsides, prohibit drilling, clean up the seas, don't be embarrassed about our shared experiences and basic truths, abandon the thought-set of fossil fuels and fear nuclear energy.

Power is Relation. That means that absolute power lies in siding with life, beauty's wholeness. It also means that all beauty is Relation.

Repetitions: "As there were nation-states, there will be relation-nations. As there were borders that separated and divided, there will be borders that distinguish and connect, and that distinguish only in order to connect."

Analysts, prophets, economists, financiers and political analysts, experts, every sort of fortune teller and scholar will agree in saying that there is a narrow, even non-existent margin, that you will fall into a crisis that has already opened up, and they won't want to grant anything more than symbolic power to you, power that is ceremonial and ephemeral, along with a brief, already worn-away period of time. But all those people would have been incapable of predicting the miracle you imposed on their expert opinions. You are a quiet thunderbolt of unpredictability, your room to maneuver lies in the unforeseeable. We are not in the same danger as you but we will accompany you. Because if every great politics is one of Relation that is also true of every art, both carry the world's cry in its clearest word and song: and so, Sir, the best of luck in Relation.

BW

MANIFESTO FOR "PRODUCTS" OF DIRE NEED[1]

Ernest Breleur, Patrick Chamoiseau, Gérard Delver, Serge Domi, Édouard Glissant, Guillaume Pigeard de Gurbert, Olivier Portecop, Olivier Pulvar, and Jean-Claude William
March 2009

The moment the master, or the colonizer, proclaims "There have never been people here," the missing people are a becoming, they invent themselves, in shanty towns and camps, or in ghettos, in new conditions of struggle to which a necessarily political art must contribute.

Gilles Deleuze[2]

This can only mean one thing: not that there is no way out, but that the time has come to abandon all the old ways ...

Aimé Césaire[3]

---

[1] Published initially by Éditions Galaade and the Institut du Tout-Monde in March 2009, the "Manifesto for 'Products' of Dire Need" is situated in the civil unrest of the widespread social protests against the high cost of living in Martinique and Guadeloupe in January and February 2009. Afterwards, the manifesto was distributed mostly over the internet, notably on the website of the Étonnants Voyageurs Festival and on Mediapart. Cosigned by a handful of intellectuals, including Édouard Glissant and Patrick Chamoiseau, it was followed by an online version in April 2009 that took up its themes and developed certain aspects of the text, *Traité pour le grand dérangement* [Treaty for Widespread Disruption]. It is necessary to add to the list of the authors of this second version – accessible on the website of the Institut du Tout-monde – the names of Miguel Chamoiseau and Danielle Laport.

[2] [Trans.] From *Cinema 2: The Time-Image*, trans. Hugh Tomlinson and Roberta Galeta (les Éditions de Minuit, 1985; Athlone Press, 1989, Continuum, 2005), p. 209.

[3] [Trans.] From "Letter to Maurice Thorez," trans. Chike Jeffers, *Social Text* 103, 28.2 (2010): 145–52.

It is in full solidarity and without the slightest reservation that we welcome the profound social movement that took root in Guadeloupe, spread to Martinique, and is now making inroads in French Guiana and Réunion. None of our claims is illegitimate. None is inherently irrational, and none is in any way more excessive than the inner workings of the system that it confronts. None can be pushed aside, neither for what it states by itself nor for what it adds to the whole of our claims. For the power of this movement comes from having united all that up until now was seen, from within the blinders of imposed categories, as unconnected and so isolated: namely, the previously inaudible struggles in bureaucracies, hospitals, educational facilities, businesses, territorial collectivities, not-for-profit associations, and all artisanal or liberal professions ...

But the most important power is the dynamic of the *Lyannaj*[4] – which is to forge alliances, and to re-forge alliances, to link and re-link, and to meld all that has been kept apart. The most important part is that the real suffering of the vast majority (confronted with a frenzy of economic prerogatives, alliances, and profits) brings together the diffuse aspirations, still inexpressible but also very real, of our forgotten and invisible youths and adults, as well as those of the forgotten others who suffer in our societies. For the most part, those who are protesting en masse discover (or begin again to remember) that it is possible to seize the impossible by the collar and to rid ourselves of the yoke of our fatalistic renunciation.

This strike is thus more than legitimate, and more than beneficial. And those who cavil, quibble, hem and haw, and are not up to responding to its challenge, diminish and condemn themselves.

From now on, behind the prosaic "purchasing power" or "household expenses" looms the essential thing that we lack and that gives meaning to existence, namely, *the poetic*. Every human life that is somewhat balanced gains structure through, on the one hand, the immediate needs of water-survival-food (in short, the prosaic) and, on the other hand, the aspiration for an expansion of the self where what nourishes us is dignity, honor, music,

---

4 [Original French publisher's note] *Lyannaj* is a creole term that designates a solidarity movement geared to distribute power across a network (like a liana, or vine, does). During the unrest of 2009, it was broadly adopted and broadcast as a symbol of the social protests against the high cost of living, and was chosen for these ends by the Guadeloupean collective Lyannaj kont pwofitasyon. The term also recalls, in a way, one of the possible meanings of the Glissantian concept of Relation.

songs, sports, dances, reading, philosophy, spirituality, love, free time spent on fulfilling our deepest desires (in short, the poetic). As Edgar Morin argues, living-for-living, just like living-for-oneself, does not open into any fullness without the concept of giving-to-live to what we love, to those we love, to the impossible feats and triumphs over obstacles to which we aspire.

"Rising prices" or the "high cost of living" are not little *ziguidi* devils that accost us without warning, or that are born solely from the imaginary thigh of some purebred *békés*. They are the results of systematic disruptions that take place after the dogma of economic liberalism takes hold. This system has taken over the planet; it burdens all peoples and it dominates all ways of thinking about the world, leading not toward ethnic purification, but rather toward a sort of *ethical* purification of all that is human – to wit, toward disenchantment, desacralization, desymbolization, even deconstruction. This system has confined our existences in egotistical and solitary lives that suppress all horizons from view and that condemn us to experience two profound miseries: to be a "consumer" or to be a "producer." The consumer works only to consume what his or her labor power produces in the form of merchandise. And the producer reduces production to the single perspective of limitless profits gained from theoretically limitless consumption.

Together, these create "anti-social socialization," in André Gorz's words, where economics becomes an end in and of itself and the rest must fend for itself. So, when the "prosaic" does not ascend to the "poetic," when it becomes its own end and begins to atrophy, we have the tendency to believe that our life goals and our need for our lives to mean something can be found in the barcodes of "purchasing power" and "household expenses." And worse, we end up thinking that the most intolerable miseries can only be feasibly dealt with through humane or progressive politics. It is thereby necessary to reimagine the products called "necessary essential items" to formulate another category of goods and services that speak clearly of a "dire need."

By this idea of a "dire need," we call on others to bear witness to the poetic already at work in a movement that, beyond all purchasing power, originates in a real, existential urgency and a truly profound appeal to our most noble instincts.

So what do we consider to be "products" of dire need?

They are everything that makes up the heart of our long-suffering desire to become a people and a nation, to enter with dignity onto the world stage, and everything that is absent today at the center of negotiations in Martinique and Guadeloupe, and soon, no doubt, in French Guiana and Réunion. First, nothing will be considered a social advance that does not lead to something more. In truth, every social advance is achieved only through political experience that learns structural lessons from what has taken place. This protest movement has made clear the tragic disintegration of our countries' institutions and the powerlessness that implicitly defines them. The "final word" or the "decisive step" is taken abroad or arrives by telephone. Emissaries alone bring competence to bear on situations at hand. Slipshoddiness and contempt haunt every step of every process. Error, blindness, and manipulation are evident in every analysis. The imbroglio of the pseudo-powers of region, *département* and prefect, just like the fiasco we call the association of mayors, has shown its powerlessness, even its breakdown, when a strong and serious declaration comes from a cultural, historical, identitarian, human collectivity, distinct from that of the governing metropole, but which has never been acknowledged for being what it is. Slogans and demands have quickly leapt above our "local presidents" to go to make their points elsewhere. Unfortunately, each social victory that is brought about in this way (in a leap above us), and that will end beyond us, will reinforce our assimilation, and thus will reaffirm our lack of existence in the world and our pseudo-powers.

So this protest movement must give rise to a political vision and a political agency capable of renewal and imagination that will provide us the means for self-determination and self-empowerment. And even if power, imagined in this way, will not truly resolve any of our problems, investing us with full responsibility will at least give us the ability to take on our problems in the future, and thus to finally deal with these problems rather than acquiescing to outsourcers. The *béké* question and the ghettoes that are popping up here and there constitute a small question that an endogenous political dialogue can solve: that of the complete restitution and the protection of our lands. It could also solve the problems of our youth. Another form of justice, or of the fight against drug epidemics, could be largely solved in this way too ... The lack of responsibility creates bitterness, xenophobia, the fear of the other, plummeting self-confidence ... The question of responsibility is, thus, a dire need. It is due to the collective lack of responsibility that persistent impasses are cropping up in the current negotiations. Granting us responsibility over ourselves would foster invention, subtlety, creativity, and the need to find endogenous, practical solutions. Granting us responsibility would transform failures and powerlessness into important experiences leading to maturation. Granting us responsibility would allow us to advance more rapidly and definitively toward the essential, whether that be in our protest movements, in our goals or in our understanding of the world.

There is also the dire need to understand that the dark labyrinth that is inextricably linked to prices (margins, sub-margins, hidden commissions, and indecent profits) is inscribed in the logic of the liberal market economy, which has spread across the entirety of the planet with the blind force of blinkered religion. Prices are thus constrained within the colonial absurdity that made us forget our own plentiful lands, local environment and cultural realities, and turned us over, naked, poor and innocent, and without *jardins-bokay*,[5] to European alimentary tastes. It is as though France had been designed specifically so it would have to import all of its food and its most commonly used products from lands that were thousands and thousands of kilometers away. Negotiations with the unfathomable chain of operators and intermediaries in this absurd colonial frame can certainly ameliorate some immediate suffering, but the illusory sense of wellbeing promised by these accords will swiftly be swept away by the principle of the "market" and by all of the mechanisms created by the noxious haze of profit schemes fed by the "colonial spirit" and regulated from afar. Bonuses, pay freezes, well-meaning adjustments, opportunistic workforce reductions and the pathetic tinkling of the excise tax cannot hold these at bay.

Therefore, there is a dire need for us to rely on the Caribbean for our vital import-exports, to think of ourselves as Americans when it comes to providing for our necessities, and for building up our capacity to provide our own energy and food. The other very dire need is to join in a radical challenge to contemporary capitalism, which is not the perversion, but rather the hysterical completion, of a dogma. The dire need is to move immediately to lay the foundations for a non-economic society, where the idea of never-ending development would be cast aside in favor of personal growth. Where job, salary, and consumption and production would be sites for the creation of the self and for the full realization of human potential. If capitalism (in its purest form, which we see today) created this Frankenstein consumer who is reduced to nothing but what is next on the list of things to buy, it also brings forth the dreaded "producers" (CEOs, entrepreneurs, and other professionals with a blindly socio-economic perspective) who are incapable of feeling anything in the face of the sharp rise of suffering and the

---

[5] [Original French publisher's note] *Jardins-bokay* are private gardens. The creole garden derives from an ancestral tradition tied to the slave era, consisting of the practice of keeping small vegetable gardens for personal use. For this reason, the creole garden is associated with the space of freedom that slaves maintained themselves on plantations, as a strategy of resistance.

overwhelming need for a new political, economic, social, and cultural way of conceptualizing the world. In this respect, there are no opposing camps. We are all victims of a vague, globalized system, which we have to confront together. Workers and small-business owners, consumers and producers, have somewhere inside of themselves this silent but ineradicable dire need that we have to awaken, the need to live life, each to live his or her own life, in the constant pursuit of what is most noble and most demanding, and thus in pursuit of the greatest fulfilment.

Which comes down to living life in all its poetic fullness

We can bring the food industry to its knees by eating new and healthy products.

We can push SARA[6] and petroleum companies into the pages of history by breaking free of all things related to cars.

We can hold at bay the water companies and their exorbitant prices, through considering each and every drop of water to be a precious commodity, to be protected everywhere, to be used the way we would use the last bits of a treasure held in our possession.

We cannot defeat or undo the prosaic while living in the cave of the prosaic. We have to open up into the poetic, humbly and soberly. None of the institutions that are today so arrogant and so powerful (banks, transnational companies, department stores, healthcare companies, mobile telephones …) will be able to ignore us.

Finally, on the question of salaries and jobs.

Here, too, we must acknowledge a dire need.

Contemporary capitalism cuts salaries while increasing its production and its profits. Unemployment is a direct consequence of the diminishing need for a workforce. When capitalism spreads beyond the local scene, it is not due to the need for a larger workforce, but rather a concern about causing the salary structure to fall more rapidly. All salary deflation increases profits, which get fed directly into the high-stakes game of crypto-currency. And so to demand a salary increase is the furthest thing from illegitimate: it is the beginning of global equity.

---

[6] [Trans.] Société Anonyme de la Raffinerie des Antilles (SARA), The Antilles Refinery Limited.

As for the idea of "full-time work," it was hammered into our heads through the needs of industrial development and the ethical imperatives that accompanied it. Historically, work was inscribed in a symbolic and sacred order (simultaneously political, cultural, and personal), which defined its scope and its meaning. Within capitalism, it has lost its creative capacity and its ability to lead to personal growth. At the same time, it became, to the detriment of everything else, both a mere "job" and the dominant organizing structure of our days and our weeks. Work lost all meaning when, having become nothing more than a sellable commodity itself, consumption became its only end.

We are now stuck at the bottom of the Abyss.

We must rescue work's poetic dimension. It must again become a site of accomplishment, for social invention and for the construction of the self, even when it is tiresome and hard. Or it must become one of many tools geared to these ends. There are many types of skills, talents, creative consciousnesses, and productive eccentricities that are being ignored today in the halls of the ANPE[7] and in the barbed-wire-less camps of capitalism's structural unemployment. Then, once we have freed ourselves of the capitalistic dogma, advanced technologies (geared toward sobriety and selective de-escalation) will help us in transforming labor-value into a sort of rainbow, transforming it from being a simple accessory tool to being an activity full of creative incandescence. Full-time work will not be linked to the production-oriented prosaic. But it will be considered in relation to what it can create in terms of socialization, in self-production, in free time, in down time, in what it can bring about for solidarity, for sharing, for aid for the neediest, for the ecological rebirth of our environment ...

It will be "everything that makes life worth living."

New types of work and civic gains will be found in what stimulates us, in what helps us dream, in what leads to meditation, in what makes possible delicious forms of boredom, in what moves us to make music, in what gives birth to adventuresome forays into the world of books, art, music, philosophy, scholarship or the dire need that opens into creation: *crea-consumption*. A poetics would say that there is no unemployment, no full-time work, no state handouts, no self-regeneration, and no self-reorganization. The sky is our limit, for all talents, for all aspirations. A poetics would say that the gross national product of economic societies reveals its brutality.

---

[7] [Trans.] Agence nationale pour l'emploi (National Employment Agency).

This is our first demand, which we bring to every negotiation table and to each subsequent meeting: that there is the principle of the freely given that should be applied to everything that would free us from our shackles, *that would allow an amplification of ways of thinking about the world, a stimulation of cognitive faculties, a means of inspiring creativity in everyone, an unfurling of the spirit that is without precedent.* This principle would signal the path toward the book, the fairy tale, the theater, music and dance, the visual arts, the artisanal, toward culture and agriculture ... That it be inscribed at the entryways of pre-schools, grade schools, middle schools and high schools, universities, and every place of learning and instruction ... That it give birth to creative uses of new technologies and cyberspace. That it promote everything that allows us to come into *Relation* (meetings, contacts, forms of cooperation, interactions, ways to wander) with the unforeseeable potentialities of the *Whole-World* ... It is the principle of the freely given that will allow venues in the social and cultural public sphere to determine the scope of the exceptions. It is in relying upon this principle that we will have to imagine the organization of the non-economic, from what must be unpaid and done for free to some reduced or symbolic participation, from public financing to individual and voluntary financing ... It is the principle of the freely given that should be the premise at the core of our new societies and forms of creative solidarity ...

Let us use our imaginations to conceive of these dire needs until the power of *Lyannaj*, or of living together, is no longer an item in the ledger of household expenses, but the infinite awareness of the full scope of what it means to be human.

Let us imagine together a political system of full responsibility, in the new societies of Martinique, Guadeloupe, French Guiana and Réunion, where they take part as sovereign powers in the planetary struggles against capitalism and for an ecologically reborn world.

Let us take advantage of this radically open consciousness so that negotiations can gain momentum, build, and then open like a flower in bloom to encompass everyone, all of these nations, which are ours.

An gwan lodyans[8] that neither fears nor abandons the powerful shivering of utopia

And so we call on these utopias, where politics will not be reduced to the administration of intolerable miseries or to the regulation of the pitiless

---

[8] [Trans.] "*An gwan lodyans*" means "a large crowd."

activities of the "market," but where politics will find again that its essence lies in everything that bestows a soul to the prosaic, while surpassing it or using it as an instrument in the narrowest sense.

We call forth a noble politics, a political art, which places the individual and his or her relation to the other at the center of a collective project governed by those aspects of life that are the most urgent, the most intense and the most disruptive, and so the most cognizant of beauty.

And now, dear countrymen, by freeing ourselves of colonial archaisms, by freeing ourselves of dependence and state help, by committing ourselves wholeheartedly to the ecological regeneration of our countries and of the world to come, by protesting the economic violence of the market economy, we are born into the world with a visibility that rises beyond capitalism and that is defined by a global ecological connection that holds the world in balance ...

This is our vision:

Small countries, suddenly at the new center of the world, suddenly grown large and powerful as the first examples of postcapitalist societies, capable of achieving a full realization of human potential within the wholeness of life ...

MSR

A POETICS OF POLITICS: AFTERWORD

Édouard Glissant and Patrick Chamoiseau have never stopped inventing a poetics of politics, using as their basis the Caribbean archipelago where our modernity, simultaneously finite, shared and commercial, for better and for worse, entered the world of relation. A politics of looking to horizons and breaking away rather than allocation and retreat. A politics of elevation and emancipation that refuses power and authority. A politics where equality is no longer an alibi for uniformity. A politics built on difference and pluralism.

Today, republished under the banner of the Institut du Tout-Monde, founded by Édouard Glissant before his demise in 2011, these four *Manifestos* and the two op-eds accompanying them show this process. Their brotherly relationship freed them to move in a joyful literary complicity beyond the present moment that was the justification for these writing. Where our imaginations have been deficient, they create a new way of thinking as they confront the challenges – whether these be social and ecological, about democracy or concerning wars or identities – that lie before us.

The first, written in 2000, thought up a way to recreate the French overseas departments that would neither copy nor prolong the dominations to which they have been subjected. The second, in 2007, was the opening call for a strong reaction against the resurgent necrosis of national identity under the banner of hatred and fear. The third, again in 2009, was an address to Barack Obama that, going beyond his election to the presidency of the United States, articulated an elevated politics in its awareness that once again humanity is on a rapid path to barbarism. Finally, in 2009 again, the fourth, echoing a social movement in the Antilles, imagined an ecological economy whereby dire necessity would be able to escape the mirages of consumption.

Showing the inextricable connection between the Whole-World and the Whole-of-Life, the relationship of humans among themselves and that of humans with nature, these four manifestos are the basis for a radical humanism, woven from empathy, fragility and precaution, all the while remaining adamant in the face of injustices and the indifference that justifies them – in short, a politics of beauty and kindness. Immediate reactions to two events – the 2005 vote for an outrageous law that extolled the "positive evaluation" of colonizations and, in 2007, the devastation brought on by Hurricane Dean – the two op-eds expanding on these subjects illustrate the stubborn concern with exchange and sharing that was inherited from the "endless sadness" and brought now by "an old land of slavery, colonization and neocolonization." "A valuable teacher," Chamoiseau and Glissant unhesitatingly write, countering the deep felt bitterness or paralyzing grievances: "Dehumanizing situations have this valuable side to them: they preserve in the hearts of the subjugated the shudder that rises to become the call for dignity. Our land is a country that most fervently desires that dignity."

Language, here, is revolution, in the sense that it overthrows, shakes up and rearranges things; it breaks shackles and at the same time it opens up possibilities. "The poet rises, and he raises the world with him," Édouard Glissant wrote about their compatriot, big brother and illustrious predecessor, Aimé Césaire, who first asserted his political involvement through a poetic rupture. In homage to "that awesome Annunciation" – the appearance of *Cahier d'un retour au pays natal* (1939) (Notebook of a Return to my Native Land, 1969) – the text that Glissant returned to in *La Cohée du Lamentin* (2005) bears the simple title "La Poésie" [Poetry].

"Poetry does not produce a universal," he adds because of his mistrust for this word set in stone that was, and still is, the alibi for dominations claiming to be its sole proprietor. He preferred the universalizable, the infinite movement of relation, those meetings and sharings where what is shared and what is different intersect, interweave and mix. "No," Glissant continued. "Poetry gives birth to upheavals that change us."

This applies also to these texts, which have lost none of their intensity or timeliness. Political though they may be in both aim and subject matter, these Manifestos are essentially poetic. They have nothing to do, however, with the hackneyed, misused and thus often unfortunate picture we have of the politically involved poet (or artist). The intertwined words of Glissant's and Chamoiseau's writing are not firmly entrenched in the posture of the poet-resistant and do not require some cause that could possibly turn into a trap, reducing the writing to an assignment, which is how René Char's works on the French Resistance and Mahmoud Darwish's writings about Palestinian camps have been seen.

Moreover, in one of his *Entretiens de Baton Rouge* (The Baton Rouge Interviews) (2008), Édouard Glissant recalled how, in the days of his youth – a time when he was deeply involved in the struggles involving the third world and decolonization – he was unwilling to use writing "as a function of inciting political action":

I thought that if one devoted writing solely to the aims of a popular struggle, a community or national struggle, and if in the work of writing one forgot what there was behind these struggles, meaning the most unobtrusive foundations of a culture, its opacities of Being and tremblings of knowledge, then the work of the writer was not being accomplished, but instead, and no less necessary, the work of a pamphleteer or an engaged journalist or militant eager to get results.[1]

By avoiding this trap where poetry goes dry and politics becomes impoverished, Glissant and Chamoiseau have opened up a new path where hope is retransformed, armed with lucidity without surrendering its radical nature. This invention works through a subversion of the language whose powerful art comes from the long time the weak spent resisting the strong, that patient impatience born of the crime of slavery. Carried off in the deep bilges of slave ships then thrown out into the totalitarian plantation system, turned into merchandise whose value did not exceed their temporary profitability, the slaves pierced that hellish darkness by creating a way of speaking that has no equal.

In the background of these Manifestos rises an imagination composed of words and sounds, gestures and meanings, representations, sensibilities, care and wisdom, holding on and restraint, humor and distance, generosity and curiosity, humanity that is both noble and simple, the entire endless, limitless universe that Glissant called "creolization." It is a creolization that, far from being reduced to its first vehicle, the creole language, transports its world of resonance and reasoning, motion and inconsistency, into the heart of other languages – French in this case. It is obviously no coincidence that the book that serves as a a guide, a sort of laboratory and workplace for his work, bears the title *Le Discours antillais* (1981) [Caribbean Discourse, 1989].

---

[1] [Trans.] Edouard Glissant and Alexandre Leupin, *The Baton Rouge Interviews*, trans. and ed. Kate M. Cooper (Liverpool: Liverpool University Press, 2020), p. 31.

This discourse is specifically one of words in motion, thoughts forming and proposals being articulated.

"All poetics imply a global politics," we read there, a guideline that Chamoiseau, in turn, would draw out with *Écrire en pays dominé* (1997) [*Writing in a Dominated Country*]. "These poetics," Glissant went on, "are inseparable from the future of peoples, the opportunity they have to participate and imagine." The discourse, consequently, is the storyteller's language rather than that of the professor. Nothing is ascertained from above, from some looming soapbox or pulpit. Speech is sharing and exchanging, woven out of shared experiences and friendly echoes, putting cultures in contact and in relation, or even better, born of things coming together and relating. "The creole language," Glissant states in *Le Discours antillais*, is literally a result of different cultures coming in contact with each other and did not exist before these contacts. It is not a language of Being but rather a language of the Related.

Therefore, one should not hesitate to read these Manifestos out loud, to speak and recite them – and preferably to a number of people. Moreover, this is how they have continued to move around, particularly through the friendly initiatives of Greg Germain, who has often lent them his voice. They are even designed for that – to be spoken rather than read – making a concrete reality of one of the promises Glissant made from his study: "to do away with the mandate that gives writing supremacy over orality" (*Le Discours antillais* again). He added the clarity that connects with what we feel in reading or in listening to them: "For us, the formally decisive element in literary production is what I would call the speech of the countryside." We find once again the feeling of not merely encountering words with their letters, their vowels and consonants, but the sense that one has discovered a physical reality that is not unknown to us, where thought sneaks in as intuition, a sort of perceptible fact.

"An neg sé en sièc." In other words, "A Negro is a century." These words, which Édouard Glissant placed as an epigraph to *Discours antillais,* are a Martinican proverb that tells of the infinitely long span of time conveyed by the great humanity produced by the Caribbean cauldron, that laboratory for the creolization of the world. Just above these words, he placed another quotation attributed to Charles de Gaulle when he visited Martinique: "Between Europe and America I see nothing but bits of dust." We can just imagine the laughter in the poet's eyes over his brainwave – bringing together these words that are as ironic as they are irreconcilable. Powerful people only seem to be strong; because they are blind, they are weak – they don't imagine these fragile places becoming forces, these islands imagining themselves into a universe, these bits of dust reinventing the entirety of the world.

And yet it is there, in that curve of archipelagos where the European West began to project its exploration and domination all over the Earth, that the paths of a liberating rebirth were charted, a new movement free from the thoughts of system that create oppressions and free from systems of thought that create submission. Yes, there, between slavery and marooning, suffering and resistance, the violence of the slave trade and the invention of freedom. These Manifestos are not content with bearing witness to the past; they announce the future with these beautiful, optimistic breakaways. They herald the century to come, over and beyond our preliminary defeats and our temporary frustrations.

Edwy Plenel
BW

Contributors' Biographies

Patrick Chamoiseau (1953–) is an award-winning author from Martinique whose penetrating and lyrical work crosses many genres while delving deeply into Creole culture. After law studies in Paris and a degree in social economics, he worked first with children in detention and then returned to Martinique, where he began to develop his theories of *Créolité*. He was awarded the prestigious Prix Goncourt for *TEXACO*, which describes the difficult interactions between structures that are imposed and those emerging from within a seemingly chaotic society. His work is noted for its humorous juxtapositions of speakers of classical French and characters whose expression is in Creole.

Édouard Glissant (1928–2011) is a writer of novels, poetry, philosophical and political essays that have significantly influenced understandings of postcoloniality. Born in Martinique, he eventually attended the École Schoelcher where he was in contact with Aimé Césaire, André Breton, and fellow student Frantz Fanon. The World War II embargo of Martinique, a sugarcane monoculture, caused starvation conditions there. Deeply marked by this time, he became politically active in the movement for independence from the continuing colonial interest of France. His work examines the effects of enslavement in the plantation world, what the enslaved people forever lost to it, and what they brought to the wider world.

Matt Reeck has translated from the French, Hindi, Urdu, and Korean. *"Muslim": A Novel*, his translation from the French of Zahia Rahmani, won the 2020 Albertine Prize. A winner of translation fellowships from the NEA and the PEN/Heim Fund, he served as the Spring 2021 Princeton Translator in Residence. He was awarded the 2020–21 Northwestern University Global Humanities Translation Prize for his forthcoming translation of Abdelkébir Khatibi's *The Wound of the Name*. He translated *French Guiana: Memory Traces of the Penal Colony* from the French of Patrick Chamoiseau with the photography of Rodolphe Hammadi.

Betsy Wing is a translator, writer, and visual artist. She has translated many works by Édouard Glissant, including *Poetics of Relation*, his early poetry, *Black Salt*, and the novels *The Overseers Cabin, The Fourth Century*, and *Mahagony*. Her most recent novel, *Now History*, is a fictionalized memoir of

World War II on the Home Front in the US. It explores how a family left behind when the men went off to fight tries to understand the horrors of war. In all three fields of practice, she follows the belief that works of the imagination are a language offering hope.

Index